The DRIVE GEAR

Engage your skills to obtain better results

JUAN G. RUELAS

The Drive Gear

by Juan G. Ruelas

ISBN: 978-1-942991-23-6

Published by:

Editorial RENUEVO

Contents

CHAPTER 1

Foreword

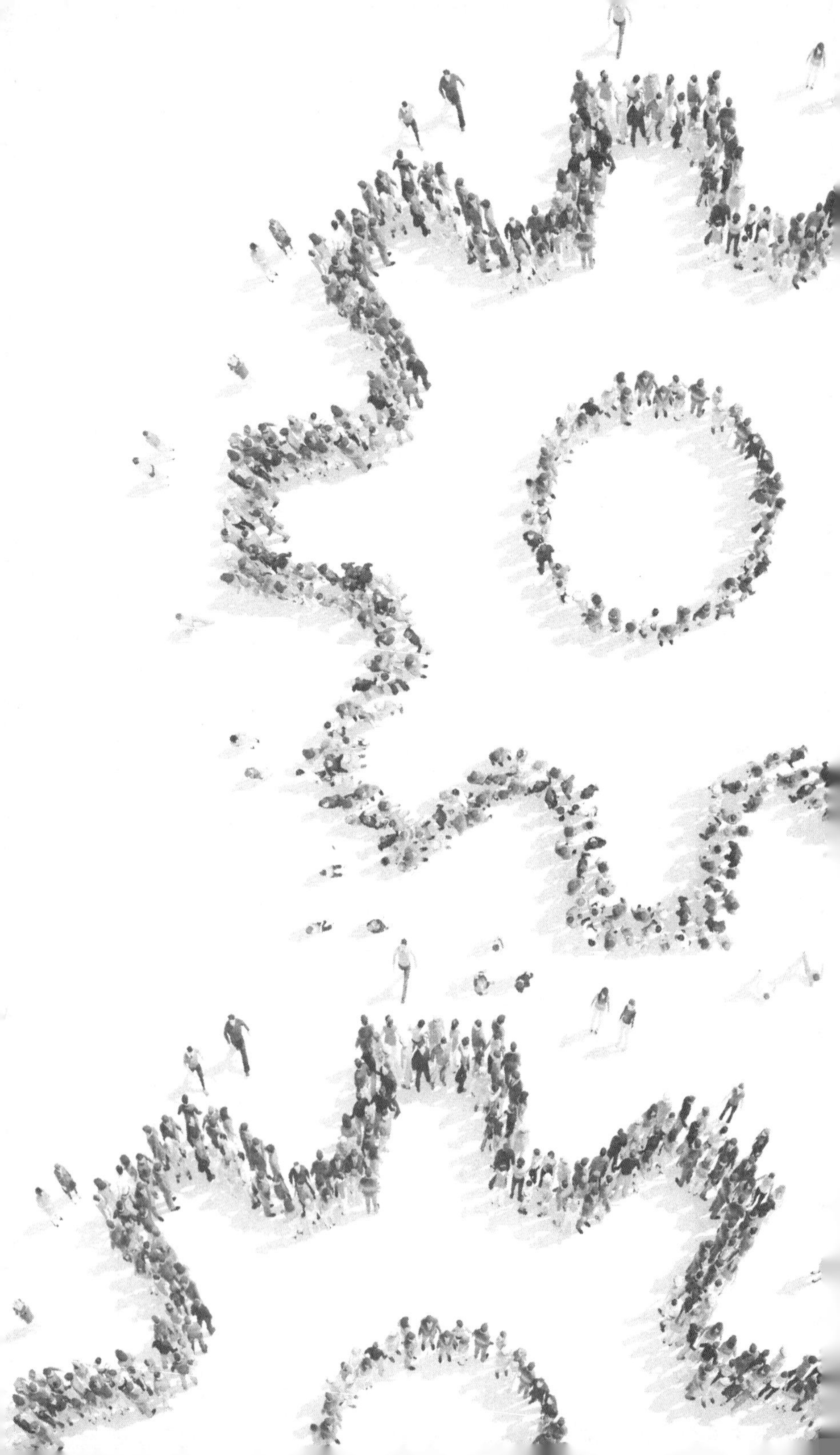

When we were introduced to this business opportunity, we began with a lot of enthusiasm, we learned about the company, we studied the products and we took on the task of learning the techniques of the business. I remember that the day after we signed up, an upline of the team came to our house to visit us. I said to him, "Tell me what I need to do to achieve results right from the beginning."

His answer was prompt: he sold me two seminar tickets, a whiteboard with a tripod and four audio tapes. Besides that, he also sold us two tickets to a business convention, two seats on the bus, and a hotel room. When he left, we had many questions. We began to attend meetings when the business plan was shown.

After seeing three presentations, we began to share the business plan. We attended trainings, seminars and conventions. For eight months we shared the business plan to our friends, family and fellow employees. No one wanted to join the business. Rather, they mocked and criticized us. Every time we commented with someone in our upline about our situation, they would recommend an audio, book, or some meeting. It seemed the business techniques were liked a jigsaw puzzle that you had to figure out in order to build the business, because no one would take the time to explain them to us.

After eight long months of arduous effort, one of my brothers got into the business. I said to myself, "If my brother doesn't see immediate results he will quit. So, we made contact with one of his friends in the town where he lived and that friend joined also. Soon, we sponsored others. After a few months there was a group of eighteen people that had joined the business.

But I didn't have experience in developing people in this business of direct sales. So I was ignorant of the personal challenges that people go through, everything from economic difficulties, marital issues, self-esteem issues, slothfulness, instability, manipulating tendencies, corruption, lies, gossip, irresponsibility and even envy.

I can remember on one occasion that one of the associates asked me to talk with his wife, because she refused to support him. He invited me to his house to talk with her. When I arrived at the house, the lady was very upset and she went to her room and didn't come out to greet us. My recommendation to this associate was the following: "You are right, you have a lioness in your house…you should leave her!" After giving that advice, I never saw that associate again.

That group of business associates that we had painstakingly formed over eight months began to fall apart. It seemed to be flawed. No one consumed products, and they didn't take the initiative to learn even the basics. They didn't attend the events and neither did they show the business plan or much less do the things they were asked to do.

I can remember saying to Alicia, "You know what? This group lacks common sense. Don't they understand what they have to do? We should start another group." Well, to not make the story too long, we decided to leave that group to fend for itself because to us it seemed defective, and we went looking for new associates in other towns.

It was in Salinas, California, three hours from Fresno, where we decided to look for new associates. One of our business partners, Juan Antonio Cruz, decided to accompany us. Alicia's first cousin lived there. For over a year we worked the business very hard in that area. We managed to establish new groups, and acquired new experiences.

The results we achieved brought big challenges for the uplines and downlines. The uplines lacked integrity—they lied a lot, they yelled at people and resorted to economic abuse of the others in the group. Many associates were affected and ended up getting out of the business. The business model made a lot of sense, but the lack of moral character, the way things were done, and not knowing how to relate to others caused that those who signed up eventually abandoned the business.

I remember on one occasion that I was worn out and very discouraged, and I asked myself, "What works and what doesn't work in this business? If I don't stop and analyze what works, we will never be able to build up this organization."

So I dedicated myself to the task of finding a way to grow in an orderly and structured manner, perceiving what was important to do, and not every man doing what was right in his own eyes. After analyzing past practices and the experiences we had lived through, I realized that all of the challenges and disagreements we had suffered were directly related to three aspects of an individual: **their form of being, their form of doing things, and their form of relating to others.**

It is fundamental to undertake a self-evaluation in these three areas mentioned. To dare to take a careful look at oneself allows the person to do a self-analysis, identifying and conscientiously recognizing our potential as well as our limitations regarding our **way of being, our way of doing things and our way for relating to others**. In other words, the success of this business model is determined by your quality of BEING, your quality of DOING, and your quality of RELATING to others.

All of the challenges and disagreements we had suffered were directly related to three aspects of an individual: their form of BEING, their form of DOING, and their form of RELATING to others.

On our way to developing this business model of direct sales and creating networks, we find people with a desire to fight for their dream while at the same time not being equipped or trained to achieve it. They were unaware of the aptitudes they need to develop to achieve better results.

It is my intention, dear reader, to share with you my experiences that may serve as a foundation to help you in building your multilevel or direct sales business in a solid and durable manner.

Chapter 2

Your way of BEING, your way of DOING, and your way of RELATING

It doesn't matter what university you attended or didn't attend, if a person wants to grow in what they are doing, needs to learn about their own way of BEING, of DOING and way of RELATING.

Simply put, lets imagine that you are standing in front of a mirror and you ask, "How am I? Do I know the methods of building this model of business? How well do I get along with others?

Setting all pride aside and exalting all that is noble is what will enable an individual see clearly what is the measure of his knowledge and what he lacks or needs to discover in order to develop and have better results.

Unquestionably, in evaluating yourself conscientiously you can only answer by what you know and not by what you don't know. Though you have to accept that there are things that you are ignorant of, being conscious of the aptitudes that you need to develop in order to be more effective will help you to channel your efforts with genuine focus.

He who dares to take a look at himself must renounce his vanity that makes him believe he is a "know-it-all". Setting all pride aside and exalting all that is noble is what will enable an individual see clearly what is the measure of his knowledge and what he lacks or needs to discover in order to develop and have better results.

In my conferences I share that life is a road that we make while we walk towards a goal or dream in a concerted manner. The things we do, we need to know why we are doing them. Why improve your way of BEING? Why improve your way of DOING? And, why improve your way of RELATING to others? Being conscious of the 'Why?' is encouraging because it gives meaning to the action that you take.

Chapter 3

Your Way of BEING

Why improve your way of BEING?

I learned the techniques of the business and the fundamentals such as how to make out a list, make contacts, show the plan and do follow-ups. The problem was not in finding people for this project. The challenge is that while you are associating people you realize that you need to fine tune and moderate your BEING.

The truth is, the people that were signing up for the business had an infinite number of bad habits. That was exasperating.

While you are associating people you realize that you need to fine tune and moderate your BEING.

Many of the new business associates were unpunctual. They had all kinds of excuses for not doing even the most basic things. There were several times we had scheduled a follow-up and when we showed up on time at the location the people would hide or say they were no longer interested in the opportunity or would come up with any kind of lie.

I soon realized that the new business associates based their potential and results on the skills or things they already knew and not on the skills or things they were about to discover, learn, and develop.

A word of advice to you who is beginning this opportunity, "What you want to achieve in life, don't base on what you already know, but rather on what you are about to learn." And to learn, you have to be available; you have to be willing, and that is when you begin to discover and understand how to do things. Availability is affected by some intrinsic human factors such as: excuses, pride, fear, low self-esteem and arrogance. A prideful person won't be moldable.

Learning begins with availability and discipline. Discipline is understood in the context of discipleship. Many times low self-esteem interferes with learning. It doesn't allow us to relax, without worry of fear of being ridiculed. We fear failure and wasting our time. We lack trust in what we need to learn. This blocks our availability. Arrogance is synonymous with low self-esteem and results in a person who doesn't know when to keep silent, or one who is shy and too silent.

Therefore, in the case of an individual who decides to start or be a part of an organization of direct sales or network marketing, it is of utmost importance that he or she understand that their manner of being impacts those who associated them, those they associated or those they are about to associate.

In other words, if their manner of being is that of being envious or dishonest, the impact on the rest will be negative. It is fundamental that a person who decides to improve or change their manner of being understand that there are a variety of manners of being to consider carefully, realizing that external results will certainly manifest themselves at a future time. So then, in regards to direct sales or network marketing, the individual need to understand what is meant by **BEING**.

The word **BEING** has multiple meanings. In a particular context, speaking of **BEING** refers to ones **personality** or **temperament**. It has to do with a psychological framework with the dynamic particularities of a particular individual.

BEING is not something acquired from the maternal womb, but rather is affected profoundly by one's **environment**, **culture** and **social surroundings** wherein each person is brought up. The way of **BEING** is that which **differentiates us from our peers** and is the result of social learning, which is related to the **habits** of each individual and the way they react to **experiences**. Our way of **BEING** is not completely formed until the end of our lives.

BEING is not something acquired from the maternal womb, but rather is affected profoundly by one's environment, culture and social surroundings wherein each person is brought up.

It is important to mention that our **BEING** is linked to our character, which in turn is composed of **psychological elements** that are **molded** with education, work, the will and the habits that allow the individual to react to his or her experiences. It is also important to note that character is closely tied to temperament and acts as a result of it in the majority of people.

Character is created by three necessary components: **emotion** (emotional impact of the individual when dealing with circumstances), **activity** (tendency of the individual to respond to a given stimulus), and **resonance** (response to events).

Our way of BEING is manifested in our actions and our relationships.

Those with a **nervous character** constantly change their interests—they get enthused or irritated easily. Nothing makes them happy. They always have something negative to say. They have no order or discipline in their lives. They tend to be weak-willed, sociable and loving. And besides that, they take all the credit.

Those with an **apathetic character** live locked in themselves, are melancholic, stubborn and lazy. They like routine and they are indifferent to their surroundings. They are apathetic and little interested in fighting for their dreams.

Those with an **emotional character** are very sensitive and pessimistic. They prefer to live isolated and they get demoralized quickly. They send to be resentful, insecure and indecisive. On the other hand, they have problems adapting to new things.

Those of a **choleric character** live busy, are bold and moved by impulses and improvisation. They are outgoing but when a problem arises they become easily stressed.

Those of a **passionate character** have a great memory and imagination and an innate capacity to work ethically. They tend to support lost causes and they are interested in learning. They are very methodical in what they do.

Those of an **insipid character** (undefined) tend to be lazy, hardly original and wasteful. They don't like to take measures of prevention, are unpunctual and nothing excites them.

My intention is not to give you a long list of an infinite number of descriptive adjectives and that you be entertained reading them, rather, to share with you the way of BEING that you need to cultivate or adjust so you can build a solid business that can be duplicated.

Our way of BEING is manifested in our actions and our relationships. Our deeds and our way of relating are a reflection of who we are inside. Therefore, it is essential that you seriously reflect on what kind of BEING you want to reflect in what you say and do. Just like an image projects out of a projector, the same way you are going to project a way of BEING. And this way of BEING will affect either positively or negatively, the goals you want to achieve.

Just like an image projects out of a projector, the same way you are going to project a way of BEING.

Here is a list of **way of BEING** that is fundamental in cultivating or adjusting in order to build a solid business, based on my experience:

1. **Honesty**
2. **Integrity**
3. **Good attitude**
4. **Honorableness**
5. **Attitude to serve**
6. **Patience**
7. **Discipline**
8. **Perseverance**
9. **Good judgment**
10. **Humility**
11. **Self Control**
12. **Punctuality**
13. **Responsibility**
14. **Respect**

1. Honesty
It is the courage to tell the truth, be decent, modest, reasonable, fair and honest. From a philosophical point of view, it is a human quality that is to act according as you think and feel. It refers to the quality with which that person is designated as shown, both in their work and in their thinking, as fair, straight and honest. He who works honestly will be characterized by the integrity with which he acts by respecting above all the rules that are considered correct and appropriate in the community in which he lives. If we apply this concept to our business then an honest partner should ask the following questions: **What is the degree of decency I feel about money? Do I practice honesty? Do I take what does not belong to me? Do I treat others the same behind their back as when I'm in front of them? Do I keep somebody else's money?**

A person who is not honest with money will not grow in business. I have seen many people come into the business and be destroyed by a lack of honesty. When they are paid for the fixed order, they take the money and spend it. Many times I observed people in my upline and downline whose real name to identify them would be Epi, who lied in order to take advantages. I perceived them as dishonest and opportunistic individuals. They were so opportunistic that when we would go to Denny's to do a verification of the progress, instead of paying for their meal they would ask their downline partners to pay the bill, for in their mind it was a privilege for the downlines to eat with them.

At other times, Epi would require his downline leaders to travel to give training without offsetting or paying for their trip. The excuse was that he had paid a high price and they also had to pay. Of course, after the event it was required that they money collected for the event be deposited to his account. Apart from this, Epi demanded that we should just build him up with the rhetoric that "he was the one who came to support us." At any opportunity he had, he would speak ill of the line of sponsorship as if he were the victim.

When we spoke with our upline, Ramon, Epi would get jealous. There were times when he said to us, "Be careful of Ramon. What a coincidence that he is developing a close relationship with you."

For a long time Epi had us believe that we had to hold our events very much separated from our "crosslines" because "we do things differently." There were several occasions when he called the Platinums to a meeting to yell and scold us. Epi loved the stage and recognition.

There were occasions when Epi sanctified his leader, Machuquis, in order to hide behind him. It was obvious that Epi's intention was to separate the group from the organization so as to make himself look like the hero. When they paid him for the fixed orders, he would take seven to eight months to deliver the products. Both of them kept what was not theirs to keep. I never observed transparency in either of them. On the contrary, they would take advantage of any opportunity to obtain personal financial gain.

An honest person is not only a blessed person, but someone who gives a feeling of security to those at their side due to the fact that honesty is what enables us to live without fear of bveing put down or scolded.

I remember when Epi would not let anyone contract the bus. He would travel from one city to another to control the hire of transportation and to charge the tickets. At the get-togethers he would charge $25.00 for having his picture taken with someone. Even though the parks were public and free, they would charge for any events where the group would get together. They not only exalted each other in order to maintain the power of influence, but they were raise the prices of the bus transportation and the hotel rooms to obtain profits by means of lying.

The level of decency of these people was very low: they kept for themselves what was not theirs to keep. This dishonest manner of BEING caused many people to avoid them. Many people left the business with a bad taste in their mouths. On the other hand, I have known individuals who are well aware of the degree of honesty they need. Juan Antonio and Dora Cruz have stood out as a couple with a lot of honesty; they are the pride and joy of Equipovision. Because of them and those like them, we can advance without fear and without major difficulties. An honest person is not only a blessed person, but someone who gives a feeling of security to those at their side due to the fact that honesty is what enables us to live without fear of being put down or scolded.

From 1 to 10 How honest are you?

1 2 3 4 5 6 7 8 9 10

2. Integrity

Integrity is about being whole within. **Something with integrity is that which is whole in all of its parts; nothing is damaged, corrupted or contaminated.**

With respect to a person, personal integrity may refer to an honest individual who has emotional control, has self-respect and respect for others. He is responsible, disciplined, punctual and pure. He is firm in his actions, and therefore, is careful, correct and does not allow himself to be corrupted. That means he doesn't allow himself to disintegrate due to jealousy, greed or temptation. Integrity, in this case, is the quality of having a moral interest, fairness and honesty in conduct and behavior. In general, a person of integrity is someone you can trust.

I could mention several who began a process of moral decay and never realized that one lie leads to another lie.

The breakdown or disintegration is a gradual process. It implies a downsizing of integrity in relation to morality. The individual in relation to honesty or any other value that characterizes it, begins to rot and decompose within. It is possible to gradually disintegrate and not realize the negative impact we cause.

With respect to a person, personal integrity may refer to an honest individual who has emotional control, has self-respect and respect for others.

The act of disintegration, of decomposition, was very common in my beginnings. Many individuals in the first organization that tried to raise up, ignored how important is integrity in this business model. Many began to deteriorate when they got involved in another multilevel model and not remain loyal to just one. Others began to get involved with other women and still others abused their leadership. They borrowed money and never paid their debts. The moral disintegration was very obvious in the organization. Jealousy and envy soon began to creep in and were part of the cause of the deterioration of an organization of around 300 individuals.

In a symbolic sense, disintegration or decomposition is associated with attacking the ideas of another person with the intention of imposing yours. For the achievement of one is the cause for jealousy of others. Those jealousies provoke and induce a bad reputation. ***Ladies and gentlemen, if someone obtains the results you desire, be*** *noble and learn. Do not let elements such as jealousy, corruption, doubt, envy, suspicion and ambitions become bacteria and begin a fermentation process where integrity starts to rot, creating pus; because eventually that rot will start to stink and your partners will avoid and stay away from you.*

The whole person is firm in his **way of BEING**. He is true to the values he professes. A person of integrity doesn't act incorrectly or what is only convenient for him, but rather does the right thing. He knows his heart, his desires, his values and knows to look inside to see if he is acting correctly and discern the motives of why acts as he acts. Integrity is always accompanied by honesty and these two are part of an integral leader. A leader who wants to guide people with lies and folly not only decomposes himself but others also. Remember that humans have intuition and can sense if you hear or see what is good or bad. Sooner or later the person who does wrong will be caught and held accountable.

From 1 to 10 Are you a person of INTEGRITY?

1 2 3 4 5 6 7 8 9 10

3. A Good Attitude

Attitude is the mood that is expressed in a certain way (as a calming attitude). Attitude also refers to the position of a person's body when transmitting something in a certain way.

In this business model, I realized that people have a way of thinking and feeling. They have some level of readiness that allows them to respond and have some level of availability. I remember when I started this business I was overwhelmed by the number of events that we were required to attend. Many things did not make sense to me because it was a repeat of the same. It seems I had to guess the why of things. My thinking, my attitude, was not molded to this kind of business, so I began to despair until I came to understand the why of things.

Just think how many people we lose by not understanding that people who we associate in this business model do not have a mind or a molded attitude to develop this business opportunity. We can be imposing, demanding and desperate, with a strict attitude if people do not do what they are asked to do. I'm sure many people are not in the organization by the attitude we take by requiring them to do something.

Ladies and gentlemen, the attitude of an individual or their thinking in relation to our business model actively **adapts to its environment gradually**, not overnight. It is a process of learning and affection. Remember, people do not care how much you know until they know how much you care for them. There is no doubt that the attitude of a person is affected by the affection shown him.

Therefore, the attitudes of human beings can predict possible behaviors. When an individual's attitudes are observed, it is feasible to provide for their mode of action and be able to influence them as a manner of guidance.

Attitudes are learned like everything in life. We grasp new information and learn new ways to make a living, and consequently develop new feelings, new attitudes and that is when we go into action. Learning is the detonator of an attitude that can be taken. The attitude is affected by the number of positive elements that have impacted the individual's mind.

Just think how many people we lose by not understanding that people who we associate in this business model do not have a mind or a molded attitude to develop this business opportunity.

People seek consistency or common sense in what they are to learn. Thus the simpler one explains things better to influence the attitude of an individual.

People do not like it when things are not clear. That affects their attitude. They feel uncomfortable when they hear things that contradict and consequently they reduce their activity. The same applies when an **action** that goes against what the person believes or is not related to what they hear. Therefore it is important to accept that reading is important to cultivate our attitude and cultivate the attitudes of others.

Keep in mind that attitudes can be changed to achieve the results we want.

It is also important to differentiate between positive and negative attitudes. **Positive attitudes** are those who work with the individual to face reality in a healthy and effective way; **negative attitudes** are those that impede the individual's relationship with his environment. The individual's freedom is in his **ability to choose** between one attitude or the other.

Finally, it only remains to say that attitudes change not only individual behavior but also that of a group. A person with a positive attitude towards the problems can encourage the group to move forward and improve, while one with a negative attitude, is able to "infect" the group and to guide them to failure.

Attitudes are learned, like everything in life.

A good attitude is one of the best qualities in the **manner of BEING** of an individual. Because **attitudes** are **feelings** that are transformed into **behavior**, we can call the attitude a quality that has a number of good attributes. A good attitude gives an appropriate image, a formal image. You project that you believe in yourself and you are willing to see the best in others. A good attitude makes you see opportunities everywhere. It motivates you look for solutions to the problems. You give without receiving anything in return. A person with good attitude is persistent, does not throw in the towel, is not afraid and assumes responsibilities. The animals are born with a spirit of survival, but humans develop their **way of BEING** and consciously adjust their attitude and that makes them succeed in life. Success or failure is not a matter of luck. It is a matter of choice to learn things that can build our attitude.

We all want to do well in life. For this to happen we must have a good attitude. And an attitude can be changed.

From 1 to 10 How good of an attitude do you have?

1 2 3 4 5 6 7 8 9 10

4. Honorableness

Honor is a **moral quality** that characterizes the individual to fulfill his own duties and have respect for others and himself. It is an ideological concept behind the behavior.

In this business model there are several shared rules that are based on ideals and what is considered an honorable behavior within a community. For example: to speak ill of someone behind their back is not honorable behavior. An instigative and manipulative attitude, moreover, violates the honor of a person.

In this organization, honor is linked to what characterizes the individual's stages of leadership: learning, doing, and orchestrating.

In addition, an honorable person is one who embraces the characteristics that distinguish a leader within Equipovision: **respects the wife of his neighbor, does not borrow money from his partners, is responsible, does not manipulate in order to be compensated, does not intimidate, does not create friction, does not change the name or re-sponsor people in order to associate them, does not lie, does not use social media to exalt themselves, does not hold clandestine events, does not charge to verify the group, does not charge to have a potlucks or get-togethers.**

Honor is linked to what characterizes the individual's stages of leadership: learning, doing, and orchestrating.

An honorable individual is helpful, keeps his word, and gains no personal benefit from the bus or hotel tickets, does not argue in front of the group, recognizes and respects the techniques of other leaders, invests in extra tools to develop the group, is fluent in the leadership model of Equipovision and gives accountability. If an individual meets all of these characteristics, he is worthy of honor and is an example to follow.

An honorable person is worthy of respect when the honorable acts that they do, speak for themselves, without need to demand that people edify him.

From 1 to 10 What level of honorability do you have?

1 2 3 4 5 6 7 8 9 10

5. Helpfulness

Dear reader, I invite you to see service as a gear, as a mechanism that promotes and enhances other individuals.

We reiterate that, "**serve**" (gear) is the name a person consciously gives to himself in reference to others, to indicate **performance**. This does not mean submission to the judgment of another or others.

Dear reader, I invite you to see service as a gear, as a mechanism that promotes and enhances other individuals.

Therefore, we must be

aware that the real gears, are true to their function (service). They **finish** their tasks, **fulfill** their responsibilities, **keep** their promises and **complete** their commitments. They **do not leave** the job half done or **abandon** it. **They are responsible and trustworthy**. Effective gears will keep a low profile. **They do not promote or call attention to themselves**. If they are recognized for their **service**, they accept it **humbly**, but do not allow notoriety to distract them from their duties.

The moral attitude of service, is not a recipe, or can be given by decree, but must be something deeper, a kind of personal habit, a kind of **virtue**, a talent of elegance that is exerted from the bottom of the heart of the person that ends up creating what is known as spirit of service or to clarify even more, such person ends up organizing the moral principle of his thought.

When we change the mindset we are changing destiny and the conditions. This will trigger a number of opportunities and circumstances that will help us open doors.

When we change the mindset we are changing destiny and the conditions. This will trigger a number of opportunities and circumstances that will help us open doors.

Talking about change seems easy, but it is not, because everything begins in the mind. Changing the images first, then proceeding to change the consciousness and behavior which in turn will change the habits. For this to happen we must begin with the mental planes. The mental attitude is conditioned by the images or pictures that we have in the mind. If we do not like the pictures, we must destroy them and replace them with others that are pleasing and are necessary for our evolution as individuals and to make this true, knowledge and awareness is required. That's where we say that everything begins in thoughts, but what people do not understand is that thoughts are first images. With art display you will begin to bring these new images and new results. Herein lies the importance of understanding the topic I am making now, because if we do not change the pictures, paradigms and mental patterns, we can never understand the greatest law of prosperity, which is based on service. **"For one who serves will be called greatest in the kingdom."**

If we do not change the pictures, paradigms and mental patterns, we can never understand the greatest law of prosperity, which is based on service.

Habits make us cling to something and if the mind is not open to review and give us new opportunities, we will act as robots and not as thinking beings.

This is the power of an image and this is the reason why people run away when speaking of service, because in the minds of people when they hear this word, the image they have is a person in subjection, a person with little or no rights, and not a person who drives or brings about improvements through his activity.

We live in a temporal world. Everything we accumulate will remain behind. However, everything we do and how we do it will have an impact on the lives of others and yes, that will remain. "When I leave this world I will not take anything material with me." Be assured that what I will take are the memories of my conduct. That will strengthen me in making the transition to a better world. "For one who serves will be called greatest in the kingdom."

In our business model being helpful is fundamental. For when you learn the basics of this business you become a mechanism for improvement and helping others. Then we come to understand that the gear is a mechanism that encourages, activates and enlivens a force which accelerates the realization of a goal.

We live in a temporal world. Everything we accumulate will remain behind. However, everything we do and how we do it will have an impact on the lives of others and yes, that will remain.

Well, thus far we have made a brief explanation of the mechanical function of "**engagement**". In this engineered business structure I propose that we perceive "**serving**" as we would a **gear**. Let's function together, organized for a particular purpose. We develop relationships at the events, our get-togethers and while at the same time planning our goals. ***Indeed to be effective in this business model we need to function in interdependence as part of a community to eventually contribute to creating other communities.***

It is surprising the number of activities that keep us connected to each other, from megaplans, trainings, seminars, conventions etc. Working together we can be more creative and effective.

We could say that we, the IBOs (Independent Business Owners), are fragments, key pieces that compose a **community** that has evolved looking for an improvement.

We could say that we, the IBOs (Independent Business Owners), are fragments, key pieces that compose a community that has evolved looking for an improvement.

We are then, individuals, pieces, fragments that form a **community** to improve our lives. We know that our capabilities and our individual resources are limited. For example, I cannot be in 100 places at the same time. Nor can I rotate the circle (List, Contact, Plan, and Follow-up) in ten different states. Neither am I so creative as to be with 50,000 people holding little schools. Neither am I an expert on technology to run more than 500 monthly events. What I don't know is greater than what I know. In fact, what I am unaware of is more than what I am aware of.

Therefore, because of my disability and my need as well as my survival, I am forced to work as a mechanism that is useful in service—to be part of a **group of individuals** marked by a common way of thinking. That creates a culture, a certain folklore, and certain shared criteria that determine our habits and lifestyle and relate to each other within a **community**. Ladies and gentlemen, to achieve the results that we desire in this business model, being helpful is fundamental.

From 1 to 10 How helpful are you?

1 2 3 4 5 6 7 8 9 10

6. Patience

Patience is the **way of BEING** that makes it possible for a human being to be able to withstand setbacks and difficulties in order to accomplish some objective.

The word **patience** describes the ability of a person to **tolerate** or **bear up** in a situation without experiencing anxiety or **loosing** his cool. Thus, we can say that patient person is one who **does not loose his cool**.

When a person or situation causes another to lose their patience, what happens is that the individual has become fed up, tired and can no longer tolerate that situation. The consequences can be varied, ranging from staying away or giving up.

Patience also represents the ability to learn to wait for someone or something without being upset during the wait. Patience is the **ability to perform different tasks or plans without letting anxiety ruin your objectives.** Patience is the **slowness with which an activity that requires precision and detail is developed.**

Patience, ultimately, is closely linked with **calm** and

peace. A patient person, according to the theoretical definition, is one who knows how to wait and takes things easy. The opposite is someone **impatient**, anxious and wants everything immediately.

A common mistake is to confuse **patience** with **passivity**, with the **lack of commitment** towards life and the obstacles of human reality. However, this is incorrect, since the first concept (patience) is a faculty that is synonymous with strength, perseverance, and often the **pillar to personal and professional development**. You cannot think of a great writer, or a recognized doctor, nor can imagine a transcendent entrepreneur who worked unconsciously and impulsively, without patience, who did not first learn about himself and his environment.

You cannot think of a great writer, or a recognized doctor, nor can imagine a transcendent entrepreneur who worked unconsciously, without patience, who did not first learn about himself and his environment.

Also, it is common knowledge that great entrepreneurs are often misunderstood by society. In many cases, coming up with an idea to improve and propose a new way of thinking or acting, instigates as a result of envy. Against this barbaric attitude, creative people (advanced) must summon courage and patience to enable, with much effort, that their ideas transcend.

Another aspect of patience is the ability to see facts and variables that may be imperceptible to the anxious and impulsive beings. For example, someone who is insulted and does not respond in an aggressive manner may seem cowardly, but it is also possible that this person understands that if he is carried away by his instincts may worsen the situation, or simply not worth getting into the game of the other person. This reinforces the difference with passivity, with lack of interest, and shows that the stronger and more active person is the one who exhibits patience.

The stronger and more active person is the one who exhibits patience.

From 1 to 10 How patient are you?

1 2 3 4 5 6 7 8 9 10

7. Self-discipline

Self-discipline is learning to be the one to manage and run your brain and not let your emotions run you. It is being able to impose rules on yourself and comply despite wanting other things at the time.

Self-discipline is when you learn to control yourself as a person without anyone else telling you. The management of discipline is a skill that allows any individual to get much more with the same effort. Someone said that if you know what you want, and you want it with enough passion, you will get it with self-discipline.

Self-discipline is learning to be the one to manage and run your brain and not let your emotions run you.

Whether you are in an emergency situation, trying to survive, or want to achieve any goal, the fact of wanting to get ahead is what motivates you consciously and unconsciously to make every effort to do so. This self-imposed conditioning is called "**self-discipline**" and a thorough understanding of this is fundamental to the achievement of any business. One thing is discipline imposed by someone and quite another thing to impose something on yourself by your own deep conviction. Imposed discipline is nothing more than that, namely imposition by force.

Discipline imposed is minimalist in that it seeks a performance or behavior that calls for toughness, while self-discipline (imposing something on yourself) maximizes, because it appeals and converts an objective into a personal need and by doing so, causes that the individuals give much more or themselves in order to accomplish to desired end.

History tells us numerous examples where, individuals who were sufficiently self-motivated, managed to succeed even in the worst circumstances, and other cases in which, despite having everything at their fingertips and all possibilities for great accomplishments, perished or were defeated. These cases have much to do with the implementation of self-discipline, as opposed to imposed discipline.

Self-discipline allows you to set a realistic goal or make a plan and stick to it. It is the ability to resist doing things that hurt others or ourselves. It involves keeping the promises and commitments we have made. It is the foundation of many other qualities of character. Often self-discipline requires persistence to meet long-term commitments or delaying gratification in order to achieve a more lasting satisfaction. It also includes knowing how to handle emotions like anger and envy, and develop the ability to be patient.

Learning self-discipline helps regulate behavior and creates from a willingness, strength and energy to make and execute good decisions. On the other hand, if they cannot develop self-discipline, this leaves them open to destructive behavior. Without the ability to control or evaluate their impulses, individuals can dive headlong into harmful situations and fail.

Learning self-discipline helps regulate behavior and creates from a willingness, strength and energy to make and execute good decisions.

From 1 to 10 How self-disciplined are you?

1 2 3 4 5 6 7 8 9 10

8. Perseverance

If you fall seven times, get up eight!

Chinese proverb

Falling is allowed. Getting up is required!

Russian proverb

It is hard to fall down, but worse than that is never having tried to climb up!

***Theodore Roossevelt** (1858-1919) American politician.*

If the seed is sown in faith and is taken care of with perseverance, it is only a matter of time to reap the fruits.

***Thomas Carlyle** (1795-1881) Historian, writer and English philosopher.*

Perseverance is the virtue by which all other virtues bear fruit.

***Arturo Graf** (1848-1913) Italian writer and poet.*

Our greatest glory is not in never having fallen, but in rising every time we fall.

***Oliver Goldsmith** (1728-1774) English writer.*

If an individual has a **manner of BEING** of persevering and not waivering, he does not throw the towel and there is no such thing as IMPOSSIBLE. Perseverance is a natural quality that occurs when you most need it. It keeps you standing in any circumstance.

Perseverance makes you observe the obstacle from where you are. Then you take the first point of support you can, and then you push off until you are standing. Trembling and sweating, but resolutely erect, muttering: "Yes, we can". Impressed by your iron will, you accept the goal. With sweat, tears and pride, you keep your word. That's when you see the perseverance materialize. It is very impressive to see a strong commitment to achieving the goal, which also trusts in that which must be done. If a thing is impossible, it will clearify itself in due time. Then all will be in God's hands, not ours. "For nothing is impossible with God." The persevering gear is durable, resistant, permanent, enduring, tireless and tenacious.

Perseverance is the **action** and **effect to persevere**. This word refers to **remaining constant** in a project already begun. To persevere is to have a positive attitude even when circumstances are adverse or the objectives cannot be met.

To persevere is to have a positive attitude even when circumstances are adverse or the objectives cannot be met.

As is known, perseverance is the key to success in most endeavors, and can be applied to diverse fields such as physical or mental work. In all cases, you should have a clear objective, a goal that justifies the effort and dedication over a generally extensive period of time.

Along the way toward meeting that goal, frustration is one of the worst enemies of every entrepreneur. So, to avoid convincing himself that it is not worth continuing to struggle, it is essential to be prepared for the failed attempts that are as natural as the triumphs.

Precisely in knowing how to accept failures as an integral part of life and turn them into resources is where the secret of victory lies. Taking as an example the study of a foreign language, it is generally believed that small learners learn better than adults, and have a lower dropout rate. The most common explanation for this phenomenon revolves around age, claiming that the younger a person is more willing to incorporate a new linguistic structure.

However, adopting a more constructive approach, we can assume that those who embark on a study as mature adults often make a mistake that children do not commit. This counterproductive element is *fear*, and originates from a constant analysis of the likelihood of failure, lack of time or lucid thinking whether it is worth investing time and money in an activity that perhaps is too much for us. Children, however, often face learning in a more passive way; they have no need to seek knowledge, it comes to them.

Perseverance manifests itself in the worst moments, just when everything seems to fall apart before our eyes. Its reward, on the other hand, is directly proportional to the anguish and desolation we feel before adopting such an attitude in regards to our battles.

Perseverance manifests itself in the worst moments, just when everything seems to fall apart before our eyes.

Given the fact that there is no possible relationship between two people in which there is never any conflict, there is no relationship that does not require perseverance to develop healthily. Drawing closer to other human beings, and even to ourselves, is one of the biggest challenges facing humanity, and one of the most enriching experiences that we can experience on this earth and, like all great opportunities, requires a great effort on our part.

It is essential to understand that it is impossible to succeed if traveling indefinitely a road that in the past has led to failure. In other words, perseverance does not consist in trying the same thing over and over again, but rather in improving the methods, trying different things, without fear of having to start again if necessary.

Perseverance does not consist in trying the same thing over and over again, but rather in improving the methods, trying different things, without fear of having to start again if necessary.

In conclusion, here is a well known phrase, "Persevere and prevail," supposedly created by the Roman philosopher, Lucius Annaeus Seneca, who was born in the year 4 B.C.

From 1 to 10 How persevering are you?

1 2 3 4 5 6 7 8 9 10

9. Good Judgment

Everything is temporal. A sensible person has good

judgment, is reasonable, serene, careful and thus has advanced understanding compared with the average. In other words, the **manner of BEING** sensible is to conduct ones self and act with intelligence. To have good judgment is be stable emotionally in everything that is done.

For example, we could mention a football player who uses good judgment when, because of his experience and understanding of the game, knows how to position himself on the field, help his fellow teammates and handle the rhythm of the game.

It is important to clarify that talent is not always linked to good judgment. A person can have much talent in one area and still not have good judgment or common sense.

It is important to clarify that talent is not always linked to good judgment. A person can have much talent in one area and still not have good judgment or common sense. Any individual can achieve good judgment from observation or attempts and failures.

My grandmother would say, "The problem is not falling over the stone, the problem is falling in love with the stone."

Good judgment, therefore, is associated with reflection, maturity, understanding. I can remember good advise that my grandmother gave me, "*You do not want to expose yourself in this way, you have to show good sense in your actions.*" On the other hand I can share with you some advise that I've shared with some leaders, "*We need leaders who manage wisely and do not squander their money.*"

Therefore, it is considered that good judgment is one of the best values that a person can have both for their own development and their relationship with others and their role in society. It is considered a key tool in dealing in an educated manner with other individuals.

It is considered that good judgment is one of the best values that a person can have both for their own development and their relationship with others and their role in society.

There are stages in which humans can be more foolish. For example, when we are learning something and totally unaware of things. We fill our head with certain perceptions and conduct ourselves in an imprudent and prejudiced manner.

From 1 to 10 Are you a person who shows good judgment?

1 2 3 4 5 6 7 8 9 10

10. Humility

Humility is the **virtue** which consists in knowing one's limitations and weaknesses and acting on that knowledge.

It could be said that humility is the absence of **pride**. In this business model I think we all suffer from some form of this lizard. Being a 'know-it-all' hinders our improvement. Being humble is a characteristic of modest individuals who do not feel more important or better than others regardless how big are their skills or their achievements.

Humility is the absence of pride.

Given the need to show our own achievements, **a certain judgment arises from those around**, and **not everyone is prepared to accept the accomplishments of others**. If we observe carefully, there are more chances that a noble mediocre actor be accepted than a proud and arrogant talented one. Even more so, if the proud and arrogant one pretends to feel close to their idol audience.

Therefore, your achievements are for your improvement, and not to make them public for that can cause envy. If you do share your knowledge, do it in secret that eventually the people you build up will let others know.

From 1 to 10 How humble are you?

1 2 3 4 5 6 7 8 9 10

11. Self-control

Self-control is to regulate oneself regarding an impulse or feeling. It could be defined as the conscious ability to voluntarily regulate ones impulses in order to achieve greater personal and relational equilibrium. A person with self-control can manage his emotions and regulate his behavior.

Self-control is, moreover, a tool that allows, in times of crisis, **to distinguish the most important (that which will endure) and what is not so important (the temporal).**

When you have self-control, you are better able to cope with difficulties. Moreover, the self-control needs **peaceful dialogue** to avoid confrontation which could result in emotional or even physical violence. **Patience** is a key virtue when the need arises for self-control.

Self-control is to regulate oneself regarding an impulse or feeling.

Individuals who accept their failures or mistakes, raise their inner balance which prepares them to accept the weaknesses and mistakes of others.

It is noteworthy that the main enemies of self-control are **irrational ideas**, causing a lack of self-worth, insecurity, dependence on what is said or done and the need for approval, for example. These ideas can even cause **depression**.

It is also necessary to emphasize that such situations can generate stress and make us lose control of our emotions and be guided by our impulses to the point that we get agitated more than perhaps is necessary.

From 1 to 10 How much self-control do you have?

1 2 3 4 5 6 7 8 9 10

12. Punctuality

In the village parish of Armatlan they were holding a farewell dinner for Father Pascual in gratefulness for his 25 years of uninterrupted pastoral work. A local politician and member of the community was invited to the presentation of the gift and a brief speech.

The politician was delayed in arriving, so the priest, to fill the time decided to give a few words himself.

"My first impression of the parish was when I heard the first confession for this town.

"I thought that the bishop had sent me to a terrible place, as the first person who confessed his sins to me said that he had stolen a television, had stolen money from his parents, as well as stolen from the company he worked for. And sometimes he was involved in the trafficking and sale of drugs. To conclude his confession, he admitted that he was unfaithful to his wife.

"I was astonished, shocked, scared to death. But as the days went by I got to know more people who were not at all like this man.

"What's more, I lived the reality of a parish full of responsible people, with values, committed to their faith, and so I lived the most wonderful 25 years of my priesthood."

Just at this time the politician arrived, so he was given the microphone to present the gift to the honored priest on behalf of the community.

Of course he apologized for being late and began his speech by saying:

"I will never forget the first day that Father Pascual came to our parish ... in fact, I had the honor of being the first to confess my sins to him."

Never be late. Punctuality is the art of not wasting the time of others. Punctuality is not a clock problem, but a problem of education and respect.

Punctuality is a fundamental mode of BEING for the individual. The value of punctuality lies in the discipline of being on time to meet our obligations: a meeting at work, a gathering of friends, a commitment to the office, delivering an outstanding work etc.

The value of punctuality lies in the fact that it equips our personality with character, order and efficiency, because when we fully live this value we are able to do more, better perform our work and show ourselves to be worthy of trust.

Tardiness speaks for itself. It demonstrates **the little or no organization of our time in planning our activities**, and of course our agenda, but what's behind all of this?

In this sense we could add how important an event is for us. If we request an interview for employment, a meeting to close a business transaction or appointment with the director of the study center, we do everything possible to be on time. But if it is an appointment with past friends, or a meeting with people in attendance who we hardly know, or with a person—who in our opinion—is hardly important, we do everything possible NOT to be on time! So what gives?

To be punctual, first we must be conscious of the fact that every person, event, meeting, activity or appointment has a particular degree of importance. Our **word** should be **synonymous of a guarantee** to count on our presence in the precise and required moment.

Another factor that hinders the experience of living this value lies in our neglect. When I observe a person who is not punctual, I am observing a person who is neglectful. Probably if I were to go to his or her house I would observe a messy house and everything that they leave for 'later'. Our lack of punctuality is evidence of our own personal inner disorder.

Let's consider how unpunctuality happens. Usually we know what time you should arrive and yet we let our imagination run away and we allow ourselves to become distracted with consciousness. Suddenly, time has passed and it is too late to remedy the oversight. That is negligence, ladies and gentlemen.

An important aspect of timeliness is to **focus on the activity that we are about to perform**, making all effort to maintain our attention focused so as not to wander and thus take every advantage of time.

To correct this, it is useful to **reprogram the neuron, understanding the important factor that this element plays in our lives**.

The worst of all this is that there are people who feel "distinguished" for their tardiness. **Being late is a way of attracting attention**. Moreover some have said, "If they really want me, they can wait," "Why be on time, if ...?" "It's okay ..." "It's always the same." These and other attitudes are a reflection of disrespect, let alone a lack of appreciation, that we feel have for people, their time and their activities.

For the **unpunctual person, there are no more excuses, pretexts or justifications**; no one believes them any more and they are devoid of all credibility for their lack of responsibility, perseverance and sincerity. In other words, a tardy gear is a defective gear that needs to be repaired or replaced because of jamming the progress of the social assembly.

We can think that maintaining an agenda and asking for help is good enough to correct our situation and of course that will make for a better life, but it is also necessary find the causes of our tardiness; those already mentioned: interest, importance, distraction. There needs to be a will to be on time, which means an extra effort—sacrifice, if you want to call it that—otherwise there will be a gradually moving away from the goal.

For the unpunctual person, there are no more excuses, pretexts or justifications; no one believes them any more and they are devoid of all credibility for their lack of responsibility, perseverance and sincerity.

It's not a matter of saying, "I want to be on time tomorrow," which would be again delaying something. It needs to be today, right now, and doing whatever is necessary to achieve it: calendar, reminders, alarms, etc.

To grow and make firmer this value in your life, you can start with these suggestions:

1) Examine and discover the causes of your tardiness: **laziness, disorder, irresponsibility, neglect, forgetfulness, etc.**

2) Establish an appropriate means to **address the root cause of your problem** (remembering that will and sacrifice required): **reduce distractions and breaks throughout the day; get up early** to finish your grooming with opportunity; **place the clock further away.**

3) Although it is somewhat tedious, write down your **schedule and plan your next day's activities.** If you have many things to attend and it serves little, do it for the next seven days. Henceforth it will be easier to include other events and can better estimate your chances of meeting it. Remember that with **will and sacrifice**, you will achieve punctuality.

Punctuality adds respect and value you. You contribute to the performance of any task. Punctuality is of those qualities that make up your honorability.

From 1 to 10 How punctual are you?

1 2 3 4 5 6 7 8 9 10

13. Responsibility

To be responsible is to add value to yourself. **Responsibility** is a **value** that is in the conscience of a person, that allows him to reflect, administrate, direct and evaluate the consequences of his actions, always on the moral plane.

The responsible person is he who **consciously** acts and is the direct or indirect cause of an event. He is accountable for his actions. He fulfills his obligations and puts careful attention in what he does or decides to share in a common set of **principles** with others.

From 1 to 10 How responsible are you?

1 2 3 4 5 6 7 8 9 10

14. Respectfulness
In a forest a man had an old hunting dog, who in his days of youth and strength never surrendered to any forest animal. The old dog, in his elderly days, found a wild boar on a hunt, and grabbed him by the ear, but could not hold because of the weakness of his body and his teeth, so in the end the boar escaped.

His master, coming quickly, was very upset, and rudely scolded the dog.

The dog looked at him sadly and said:

Master, my spirit is as good as ever, but I can not rebuild my old age let alone my strength. I prefer you to praise me for what I have been, and not mistreat me for who I am now.

Respect is the regard for something or someone. Respect is a value in and of itself. The term is used in reference to moral and ethical matters.

Respect in interpersonal relationships begins in the

individual, in recognition of it as the only entity needed in order to understood one another. It is knowing how to value the interests and needs of another individual.

Respect is a value that allows a person to recognize, accept, appreciate and value the qualities of others and their rights. That is, respect is the recognition of self-worth and rights of individuals and society.

Respect allows society to live in peace, in a healthy coexistence based on rules and institutions.

Respect is not only manifested towards individuals or laws, it is also expressed toward **authority**, as in the case of students towards their teachers or children towards their parents.

Respect allows society to live in peace, in a healthy coexistence based on rules and institutions. It means recognizing the rights and obligations of oneself as well as others, so often summed up in the phrase, "Do unto others as you would have them do unto you."

Conversely, **disrespect** leads to violence and confrontation. When this fault has to do with the violation of a rule or a law, it is punished even at a formal level. This punishment can be an monetary fine or even imprisonment.

Many, and of varying severity, are the acts of disrespect that exist within our society. For example, there are those committed within the workplace when the boss does not treat his workers as human beings but as slaves. However, it can also take place within the family when the children yell at their parents.

Rudeness, lack of tolerance for ideas or lifestyles of others, lack of values, pride and self-centeredness are some of the elements that most often originate such disrespect. They are increasingly common in areas such as, for example, where education has increased the number of students who face and insult their teachers.

Better to have the respect of others, than their admiration!

Remember, what you respect you draw to you. What you criticize, you push away from you.

Honor to whom honor is due!

Better to have the respect of others than their admiration!

Respect for the rights of others is peace!

Respect is a value that is not inherited, it is acquired!

From 1 to 10 How respectful are you?

1 2 3 4 5 6 7 8 9 10

Evaluation:

Total Points # ________

126-140 = Your **manner of** BEING is EXCELLENT!

114-125 = Your **manner of** BEING is ABOVE AVERAGE.

99-113 = Your **manner of** BEING is AVERAGE.

1–90 = You need help.

CHAPTER 4

Your Way of DOING

He who doesn't work on his BEING, will fail in his DOING. DOING is a reflection of your BEING.

DOING is simply the ability and the manner of putting into practice the things that need to be done. For this reason let us say that according to this model and elegance of putting into practice the things that need to be done you will be observed, perceived and duplicated.

Therefore, the individual has to be careful that his actions will motivate duplication, because to be imitated or duplicated by others soon will demonstrate if there are tangible results.

DOING is a reflection of your BEING.

At the beginning it was difficult for me because the people who associated us had no notion of how crucial it is to model things before prompting someone to do something. I remember the third day after we signed up that Alicia showed the business plan without prior training. A week after we started the business I scheduled a meeting to present the business information. I asked my sponsor to accompany me so I could observe his presentation.

Upon arrival at the location and setting up the white board, my sponsor told me that he had just come with me to accompany me and that I should give the business information. Without an outline to follow and without any previous training I gave the presentation and to this day I remember that I failed to even get the attention of the people in attendance.

For eight months I did presentations without any results. I listened to audio tapes, went to events and still could not get anyone to sign up for the business. There were times when I asked myself, How am I doing things? How could I improve? I gave myself the task of observing and analyzing how the presentations were given. I began to put order to my presentations: daily routine, business plan, dreams, close. I began to copy and tell the best stories and jokes in order to relax and inspire the possible prospects.

Before long, we began to associate people and they had the same challenges as I had. Many gave up. We would associate a number of families and the first month or two they would abandon the business. It was very frustrating to see people give up. But still we did not understand why they were quitting.

After a while we realized that before people can do something they first have to learn what to do. So we created a concept of small schools, which consisted of meeting in the house of one of the new partners and begin a process of training in relation to everything the new associates had to do in order to get results. We knew we had to model the process of association before the partners could put it into practice themselves.

After a couple of trainings we realized that people needed

not only to be trained but also needed to be strengthened mentally before exposing them to putting what they learned into practice. We took on the task of helping to raise within them the conviction that they could be successful people. It was necessary to remove the excuses and lift their self-esteem. No individual can succeed without first believing. Therefore work on the individual's **BEING** is essential. **BEING** affects **DOING**. That is, your inner knowledge and the way you feel in relation to this business model have a direct impact at the time of executing the action necessary. So, ***whoever does not work in their BEING is destined to have failures in the DOING***.

Whoever does not work in their BEING is destined to have failures in the DOING.

If it is true that no individual can obtain positive results without first working on his BEING, in the same manner no individual can get results without working on the DOING. There is no success without the quality of DOING what has to be done. How much you know, how honest you are, how upright, patient or responsible you are, it is all useless if you are not able of DOING. Nothing happens. You know everything, but you do nothing. It is essential to understand that no matter who you are or how much you know, you'll never stop improving. The first most important step is: you have to learn. The individual learns through what he sees and hears.

After watching and listening, humans have the ability to imagine things and after imagining what he saw and hearing, he will do it. Therefore to evaluate the effectiveness and monitor the growth of an individual in this area of endeavor it is necessary that those who are undertaking this business model consciously acknowledge the areas that must be cultivated in order to do things effectively. In my exprience, tasks to be developed and monitored in order to be effective are:

1. **Accept responsibility**
2. **Work ethic**
3. **Availability**
4. **Tenacity**
5. **Persistence**
6. **Dream**
7. **Commitment**
8. **Implementation (List, Contact, Plan, Follow-up)**
9. **Plan**

1. Accept Responsibility

Responsibility is the ability to meet your obligations, that is, if you committed to do something, you do it and don't make excuses. If you are a person who just started this business project you must assume the responsibility to strengthen your mind. If someone provides audio CDs, listen to them. If they lend you books, read them. One must accept the level of leadership they are in and take the responsibility to move to the next level. If you are at Level 1, that is, if you're just learning the basics of this business, apply yourself to learn like you have a debt to pay. Make your priority learning.

If you committed to do something, you do it and don't make excuses.

Practice how to draw up a list, make a contact,

then present the plan and do the follow-up. Strengthen your mind through audios, books and events. Raise your level of conviction and eliminate all excuses. Attend the little schools and allow yourself to be moldable. If you are at Level 2, if you know the basics of this business, and you already associated a person, have the responsibility to drop down ten levels in depth while that person learns. Train the newcomer. Model the things the new associate needs to learn. Read to learn how to inspire others to fight for their dreams.

Accept, as an indebted person, your responsibility, that for no circumstance whatsoever, are you going to put off for tomorrow what you need to take care of today, be that in regards to your personal growth or being out "in the trenches".

The responsible person is the one who understands and consciously acts on that knowledge that he is directly or indirectly the cause of what he learns or does.

As individuals it is important to make demands of yourself. Ask yourself how you are doing in reading: Are you unreliable? Are you immature? Are you lazy? By self-analysis you were gain a clear and real picture of yourself in order to focus on the areas where you need to grow.

The responsible person is the one who understands and consciously acts on that knowledge that he is directly or indirectly the cause of what he learns or does. He is obligated to answer for his actions, fulfill his obligations and be careful and pay attention to how he does things and makes decisions.

From 1 to 10 How well do you accept responsibility?

1 2 3 4 5 6 7 8 9 10

2. Work Ethic

Having **work ethic** is to have a certain level of human action. You decide how hard and with what kind of quality you do things. He who has a good work ethic, does things with valor, is courageous, brave, tempered, cheerful, released, passionate, resolute and determined.

Having work ethic is to have **breath** or force in the implementation of the action. For example, *"An individual with good work ethic is needed to model the curriculum of Equipovision."*

Work ethic is associated with the value that you assign to the things you do and the effort you want to put in to doing it. When a person has a good work ethic, they are able to overcome their fears or concerns and act decisively and firmly. Good ethics is demonstrated in the great acts but also in small daily actions, for example, from associating someone and starting to train them, to leading an organization. To speak the truth, it is necessary to have good ethics.

It is possible to understand work ethic as a courageous and voluntary action. He who has a good work ethic draws strength which ordinary people do not have and ends up doing things that others are not willing to do.

Specifically, there are many examples of leaders in Equipovision that because of their work ethic have made historical events and have contributed to the exponential growth of the organization.

Particularly among the most significant are those that believed when we were just a small group. Thanks to the courage and the faith of some of the DOERS, we enjoy their testimonies and experiences that have become the tools that we use today to raise the business.

Similarly, thanks to the ingenuity and the early leaders, Equipovision occupies a very desired place in the direct selling industry.

The work ethic of Equipovision condemns a number of things; just to mention a few:

1) that a leader get involved with someone else's wife;

2) borrowing money from downlines;

3) changing the names of people in order to sign them up, or changing the line of sponsorship;

4) planning and holding clandestine events not approved by Equipovision... etc.

It is by protecting the principles and ideals of the community that you represent an ethical person.

It can be said that good work ethic is the human virtue to pursue an initiative despite the difficulties and impediments that present themselves. These obstacles gender fears that are overcome by an ethical way of BEING and a committed desire to do things right.

The opposite of work ethic is laziness.

The opposite of work ethic is laziness. The good-for-nothing, therefore, has no courage or energy to accomplish the tasks and overcome the difficulties. ***I have always believed that there are people with a high level of work ethic in Equipovision, but the behavior of some weak leaders shows me that there are also large lizards and cowards in this community.***

From 1 to 10 How great is your work ethic?

1 2 3 4 5 6 7 8 9 10

3. Availability

Availability is to be willing with a positive attitude to be part of something or accomplish something. Within our business model it is very common when someone signs up or is starting the business, to be the type that needs to be begged to do something. One has to plead with them to listen to audios or attend events in order to begin a process of growth. When a person is pressured by much insistence, they may become tired because things become a burden and they begin to despair.

A clear example is the new members who have not raised their commitment level to learn the basics of this business. They themselves cause a delay and hindrance to their growth.

In a certain context not being available to learn the basics is considered as an act of contempt and not respecting the time and effort of others. ***So, New Partner, be thankful, shake off any laziness and be available to learn from anyone willing to teach you.***

On the other hand we have partners who are not so new; those who already know the basics to develop their business. They may have associated people in their line but there are too lazy to model by example how to do things. They don't have the ambition of setting an example and going down five levels deep.

In many cases the unwillingness to do something is because they compare themselves with others and decide they are not going to work harder than anyone else. It is important to realize that when you know something and the more you do the more you have results. That is, if you invest your time, you get something in return. If you waste your time you do not get anything in return. The availability of a leader, to do what others are not willing to do, is the main tool that he has in setting an example and modeling for others. You could say that availability is the basic principle that distinguishes and raises a person above the rest, because it is known that you can always count on him.

So, New Partner, be thankful, shake off any laziness and be available to learn from anyone willing to teach you.

Jose Marti, (addressing his companions in the struggle for the independence of his country, who complained of improper attitude and lack of availability of some of its members) in one of his letters said to them: "Do not be afraid of bad attitudes of others, because there will always be many men without decorum, but always one with the decorum of all."

I must mention that we have in Equipovision, Ricardo and Claudia Zermeno, who personify **availability**. They are a good example and ensure it with their good behavior, their moral standards, their actions and behavior in their work with their partners and the deployment they have with their teams which allows me to decorate and distinguish them as an example of Availability. With this virtue, Ricardo and Claudia inspire confidence to ensure assistance and support for its members. Equipovision knows it can count on them to continue taking this message of prosperity. Thanks, Ricardo and Claudia, for your availability and willingness.

From 1 to 10 How available are you?

1 2 3 4 5 6 7 8 9 10

4. Tenacity

Tenacity has the quality of elasticity. The elasticity is resistant and stands up to breaking. The tenacious individual who joins this business opportunity is firm in his decision. He has the power to stretch. For even after working at his employment or fulfilling his commitments in his daily life, is still willing to strive to learn new things and develop new skills to improve his lifestyle. No matter how tired he is after putting in a day at work, the new business partner is stretched. He attends events, reads, listens to audios, and practices the basic steps that are going to build his business. Tenacity makes you feel the warmth of your effort; you break into a sweat without breaking you.

Tenacity absorbs frustration and gives you the energy to resist when you are stretched. Like on the occasions that a new partner who is enrolled in the small schools meet at night to practice the basic steps. Probably you come home tired but determined and with a display of flexibility to stay on track. Because when the going gets tough, those who are tough (capable of stretching) remain on the road.

When the going gets tough, those who are tough (capable of stretching) remain on the road.

If you have been some time in the business and are on the second level, that of DOING, your tenacity is to not push anyone to do what needs to be done, but to pull them up and lead them by example. You need to be flexible with your partners and adapt your schedule while you build them up. Reading is essential to learn how to build your group.

Your tenacity depends directly on how strengthened and how convinced you are that you are able to build an organization. You will be tested. Just remember that things do not always go well and as you keep trying over and over and over again, eventually you will improve and you will achieve positive results.

Your ability to handle rejection without suffering damage or break-up of your dreams is what makes you distinguish yourself from others. Therefore, toughness is an attitude characterized by resistance to adversity. A tenacious person is firm and insistent in their attitude, conduct or behavior to achieve his goal.

Tenacity is acting with passion, confidence and flexibility. A person can fail many times but if he is willing to learn from his mistakes and keep trying, it is very likely he will reach his goal.

Many believe that toughness is a prerequisite for success in any field of life. In the expression, "Whoever will triumphs must never abandon!" the importance of remaining standing, trying again and again to make dreams come true. At the same time, has an implicit meaning that the real failure lies in giving up, to stop fighting.

If you could measure the magnitude of perseverance and determination that a person demonstrates in pursuing their goals before giving up, then the resulting value would be his tenacity.

Some people mistakenly assume that tenacity requires a series of particular **virtues** that not everyone has. But on the contrary, a tenacious attitude demands the use of 100% of our abilities and energies to achieve an objective. **Tenacity is the ability to withstand the blows of life without allowing them to break us down or make us quit.**

Typical failures and disappointments of life in this world leave us wounds, often indelible, and it is up to us to get up and keep moving to avoid being emotionally destroyed. If you could measure the magnitude of perseverance and determination that a person demonstrates in pursuing their goals before giving up, then the resulting value would be his tenacity.

From 1 to 10 How tenacious are you?

1 2 3 4 5 6 7 8 9 10

5. Persistence

Persistence is the **action and the effect** of remaining constant in something; to last for a long time. Persistence is considered a very important value to achieve a goal or reach a goal. Equipovision leaders recognize a number of components in order to achieve the desired results such as, investment of time, planning capacity, strategy development, intrapersonal intelligence, strategic knowledge etc., and also recognize that persistence as a key element for success.

This attitude and personal skill helps make up for the lack of other skills. A persistent person keeps trying despite their seeming lack of knowledge and the inevitable failures and can learn from each of them. Persistence is linked to overcoming obstacles, no matter how difficult they may be.

New Partner and not so new, as put by one of the leaders of Equipovision, "Persistence is the key to success". Ramón and Rosy Hinojos pursue this principle and maintain their presence 'in the trenches' with the slogan, "Persistence is the key to success". They are always behind each of the partners Equipovision encouraging and showing them that "Yes you can!" Ramon and Rosy are persistent in sowing dreams and their years of quality leadership makes them examples to emulate.

Persistence is the key to success.

From 1 to 10 How persistent are you?

1 2 3 4 5 6 7 8 9 10

6. Dream

Imagination is greater than knowledge. Listen to what your heart cries out. Expose yourself to the possibilities of things. Use your senses to experience the possibilities. For example, take yourself so you can touch, to see, to taste, to drive and take pictures of what you want.

The purpose of a dream is to focus on what we want in our lives and give meaning to our efforts. If we are to run a certain distance, we need to know why we are going to run. We should know in advance what is the reward at the end of having traveled that distance. The reward will keep us focused. Perhaps you will do business with the end in mind to get some of the following rewards: pay debts, education for your children, help your parents, etc.

For there to be steady progress, it is necessary to understand how goals are achieved. Your dreams can be just a fantasy, an illusion, if they are not equipped with the following items.

The purpose of a dream is to focus on what we want in our lives and give meaning to our efforts.

Keep a plan of how you will achieve your dream based on short term as well as long term goals. The goals will keep you in the game. Remember a goal that does not incite to action, is not a good goal.

Talk to yourself with words that encourage you to keep moving forward. Inject life into your business, visualizing yourself great. Fix your eyes on the target and get to work! We can not hit something we can not first see!

From 1 to 10 How great do you dream?

1 2 3 4 5 6 7 8 9 10

7. Commitment

Desire loses its value if we do not give it a sense of urgency. Self-commitment will provide a strong continuous focus. Handle daily the decision you made to do this business. Be full of emotion and passion so that what you want to achieve will of itself put pressure on you. Fall in love not only with the chance of getting what you want to achieve but also with the fact that you are willing to pay the price.

Success is not on sale, nor will it ever be so pay the

price to obtain whatever it is you want to achieve. Nothing worthwhile is achieved without effort and sacrifice. Here, no one will obligate you to do your part to grow your business, but the results you want to achieve, they will put demands on you. The purpose of commitment is that it leads to a state of mind and to adopt the attitude of doing what you have to do, and make a personal promise to achieve your dreams in life.

The purpose of commitment is that it leads to a state of mind and to adopt the attitude of doing what you have to do, and make a personal promise to achieve your dreams in your life.

There are five indicators that will show the level of commitment that you have with your business:

1. Listening to audio materials

How many CDs do you listen to, daily and weekly? How many do you go back and listen to again? How many do you share with others? Learn from the experts. Knowledge and experience lead to belief, and belief will lead you to action and action will bring results.

2. Reading books

How many books do you read in a month? How many books do you go back and review? How many are you sharing with others? Reading will help you to have a better self-image. You will learn principles of success that you can apply to your business. Besides, you will obtain practical wisdom that you can put into practice on a daily basis.

3. Attending the events

Attend all of the events put on by your organization. How many events do you attend? How many people do you take with you as invited guests? On a regular basis set goals with the person you are guiding. By participating in the events, you allow him to associate with successful people in this line of work. He will learn from those who are actively developing the business. This will give him more confidence when he puts into practice the techniques he learns in the audios.

4. Using the products

Do you use the products every month? How many people do you help to set up their monthly product list for their own use. Become your own best customer by using and commercializing the products of your own business. Earn money right away! To learn ways of presenting the products and techniques to commercialize, plan to attend product-training events that your team will recommend to you.

5. Staying in the game

Keep up the activity. How many times have you cycled through the four steps for business growth: List, Contact, Plan, and Follow-up? Do you do that weekly? Monthly? Draw up a plan of action on paper and make it happen. Be sure to set a good example for your team. Cycle through the four steps (List, Contact, Plan, Follow-up) at least 15 times a month. Be a Key Doer!

Start to rotate the cycle as soon as possible. While you are being trained by the system your presentations will improve. Begin right away, it's worth it! You will help a lot of other people improve their lives and as a result you will make your life better also.

Success is directly related to the commitment you have with achieving your dream. It is a personal decision as to the time you are willing to dedicate to your business. Keep in mind that the most important thing is to be consistent.

The greatest danger that you can expose your business to is inconsistent and sporadic effort. Maintain firmly in your decision to do what needs to be done. In order to accomplish this, it is important for you to fix goals because success is hidden in your daily routine. Do things according to what you want to achieve or things that keep you from what you desire.

Take advantage of the development program of your organization. This can accelerate your personal and professional development.

From 1 to 10 How strong is your commitment?

1 2 3 4 5 6 7 8 9 10

8. Implementation (List, Contact, Plan, Follow-up)
No individual can be successful without the ability to implement what he has to do. It matters little how much you dream, or how responsible you are, or how available you are, or how persistent you are, or how honest you are as a person of integrity, or how patient you are, if you are not capable of implementing what you have to do.

And so, to evaluate the growth of your business it is necessary that you are conscious of the areas that you need to implement in order to do things effectively. In my experience, the areas that need to be implemented in order to be effective are the following:

1. Write down a list of names – family, friends, colleagues and others. Think of family members, people from church, your work or friends you socialize with. Look for those with whom you have certain influence. Write down names and prioritize them.

The greatest source of people are strangers that we would like to win over as friends. Identify those who have a dream and are hungry and ready to fight for their dreams. These are your best candidates. They have a greater advantage over those who are content with life as is. Don't prejudge anyone. Dedicate a good amount of time making out your list of all of the people that you know, either professionally or casually.

It matters little how much you dream, or how responsible you are, or how available you are, or how persistent you are, or how honest you are as a person of integrity, or how patient you are, if you are not capable of implementing what you have to do.

Remember that strangers are just friends that we haven't met yet. Give priority to these names in relation to their ambition, and see who you can identify with. Remember, the mind stores names according to categories. Consider remembering names not only by appearance but rather by the amount of attention they show when you present them the business plan.

The purpose of this list is to put people on The List, and take them off of The List. See the Prospect List to obtain more information regarding how to develop your List of Names.

The ASSETS of your business are people. The INVENTORY is the List of Names.

2. Contacting - How do you contact a stranger? You don't contact him—you make him your friend. Perfect the art of being kind, positive and pleasant. Make the necessary time to interest yourself and get involved in the lives of others. Make them feel important and comfortable with themselves by listening to them and making positive comments about them.

Let people get to know you and trust you. Remember, the favorite topic of conversation for everyone in the world is, themselves!

The purpose of the contact is first of all to get to know someone unknown, to talk and get to know one another better (acquire information). The purpose of getting acquainted is so as to awaken an interest (curiosity) and to be able to show them the Business Plan.

a. **Interview** - Learn to listen attentively and to be a good observer. Ask interesting questions and listen. People will give you the opportunity that you need to present the business.

b. **Relax and trust in yourself** – Visualize people as if they are already in the business or that they want to be in the business.

c. **Frequent and cultivate** – By frequenting the same places (the same restaurant, the same supermarket, etc.) Make an effort to get to know and interest yourself in people. There are prospects all around you.

d. **Use the appropriate approach** – Never deceive, exaggerate or come across as a sales merchant, rather as a business person.

e. **It is important to have a professional appearance** at all levels of building the business, but especially when making contacts.

f. **Make sure that the prospect understands** that it is about acquiring information. Never beg or pressure people to see the Business Plan.

g. **The prospect needs to know all along** that it is about a business. Don't approach people in a chaotic, enigmatic or mysterious manner.

h. **To begin with,** awaken their curiosity.

i. **The less time you spend talking,** the better the results.

j. **Keep from discussing the details** of the Compensation Plan as this will diminish curiosity and the result could be a premature decision.

3. Show the business plan - Give life to dead time and start your success. Nothing happens until you show the Business Plan. Organizing and conducting your meetings is the best way to expose your prospects to the Business Plan.

There are a variety of ways to show the business plan with others, such as personal interviews, or one on one, home meetings or Open Meetings where the Business Plan is shown.

The purpose of showing the Plan is that people begin to dream, and this business is the best way for them to achieve those dreams.

When you show the plan, focus on the following points:

a. **Identify the dream** – Discover what they want and place this business opportunity next to their dream.

b. **Take the time to get to know them** – Identify their personality type and speak in a manner that they can relate to you.

c. **Begin making a list of names** – Get them to begin to think of people they know and to write their names down on paper.

d. **Schedule a meeting** – Agree on a follow-up meeting so you can encourage their interest and help them begin their own business.

e. **Send them home with materials** – Make sure they leave with materials right from the first meeting they attend.

REMEMBER...

Those who show more plans, have more success!

4. Follow-up - See the people again for the purpose of helping them begin the business. Success in this business begins with a personal relationship. If you show the Business Plan without scheduling a Follow-up session, you are letting go of a potential leader.

The synchronization of the follow-up is very important in order to achieve success. Of all of the steps that are involved in building a successful and productive business, the follow-up is without a doubt the most important and is used in every step of the Seven Steps of Success.

During the follow-up session, try to get to know them a bit better. Explain to them the next steps that they need to follow; never assume that they know what they must do. Remember that it is more about showing them how to get what they want than about how to do things.

The purpose of the Follow-up is to get the new prospect to become an active member with you and the rest of the team.

a. Let them get to know you and feel comfortable with you and trust you, as you focus on them.

b. Focus on their dream. Get them to re-focus their attention on their own dream and then place this business next to those dreams.

c. Answer their questions. Offer information so they can continue taking the next steps and begin to build their own business.

From 1 to 10 How good are you at implementing?

1 2 3 4 5 6 7 8 9 10

9. Planning

Develop strategies to get what they want to achieve. Have you ever seen an architect build something without first drawing up the plans? Of course not!

The same applies to you if you want to build this business. The first thing you have to do is plan. Set goals, put the action, evaluate your results and make adjustments. Remember that the plan how to reach levels is very much like wanting to build a house. You need plans (a blue print).

A) Establish strategies and consult with your guide

Evaluate the progress. Set goals, put into action, evaluate the results and make necessary adjustments, with the help of your guide, is very important. Give preference to the leader who is active and growing in the business; it is of vital importance for his success.

B) Build relationships

No one really cares how much you know until they really feel how much you care. The new business partner is concerned about his goals. If you are going to be his guide then take an interest in the goals that the new prospect has. If you are a new business partner, count on your guide in order to benefit from their input and reach the levels that you desire. In him you have someone you can get advice from and get your questions answered.

C) Draw your group

D) Develop strategies

Develop strategies as to how and when to work most effectively and how to create volume in the business so you can qualify for promotions.

1. Establish goals as to how many people to associate and where.

2. How many times did they break the cycle of **List, Contact, Plan, and Follow-up?**

3. Establish who has reached the second level of leadership (DOING) so they can develop the width.

4. Talk with them about the new IBOs they have signed up and plan to connect them to the system.

E) Match your efforts and results with the Plan of Action

F) Don't be a Chameleon Leaders: that at the time for action, you change color!

G) Sharpen your axes with the Training System

1. Listen to audios, read books and attend events.

2. Establish goals as to how many you will connect to the system.

From 1 to 10 How well do you plan?

1 2 3 4 5 6 7 8 9 10

Evaluation:

Total Points #__________

81 - 90 = Your **manner of** DOING is EXCELLENT!

72 - 80 = Your **manner of** DOING is ABOVE AVERAGE.

63 - 71 = Your **manner of** DOING is AVERAGE.

1 - 62 = You need help.

CHAPTER 5

Your Way of RELATING

John Maxwell says that leadership is influence. Knowing how to influence others is to know how to relate and connect with them.

Relationships reflect the tie that you have with people—the link, connection, familiarity, and what you mean to them. People don't care about how much you know until they know how much you care about them. People want to know if there is synchrony between what you say and what you do. Your BEING and DOING are interconnected. This is one of the greatest challenges of relationships because it is possible you can say a lot, but do little. Your way of life is reflected in your DOING. And, as they say, between the cup and the lip there is many a slip. This is the way you gain the confidence and trust of the people and that you build meaningful relationships.

People don't care about how much you know until they know how much you care about them.

No one can achieve success alone. To relate to someone is to connect with another person. By relating, we mean the ability to get along well with others and form lasting friendships with people. When one connects through an idea or project, this facilitates the connection to work together. Having points in common and engaging in ways of doing things is essential for a good relationship.

By having an inclusive attitude, relationships within our business are molded. The person who seeks not only their own personal benefit but also the benefit of those around him, tends to raise their level of companionship. Similarly cultivating close communication among those around you allows you to improve relationships.

In this business model, being a liar, having a lack of integrity, bad attitude, being lazy, impatient, undisciplined, foolish, arrogant, unpunctual, and disrespectful, affects relationships.

In this business model, being a liar, having a lack of integrity, bad attitude, being lazy, impatient, undisciplined, foolish, arrogant, unpunctual, and disrespectful, affects relationships. Similarly not accepting responsibility and not having a good work ethic and not knowing how to do things affects relationships with your downlines.

The quality and quantity of relationships that you maintain will be the extent of your leadership. If an individual does not aspire to expand his relationships he cannot achieve great things.

A team is stronger than an individual. It is essential that an individual be constantly measuring the active working relationships within his group, all the while cultivating new relationships as their constant goal. It is obvious that the difference between an Emerald and a Platinum is the amount of active relationships that each maintains.

Therefore, it is essential for the leader to register a directory of the people associated with his group with the purpose of raising the personal touch. In this manner it is possible to develop relationships by raising personal appreciation that will establish healthy, positive, and lasting relationships.

Good relationships lead to working well as a team. It allows multiple individuals to do their part with a common goal with enthusiasm and encouragement to run.

Working as a team is one of the conditions of work that has a positive psychological influence on the individuals that allows for friendship.

Good friendships give very good results, as it usually generates excitement and satisfaction when accomplishing the recommended tasks.

Good relationships also foster an atmosphere of harmony. Camaraderie is achieved when there is friendship.

Therefore, the leader has to start by measuring his ability to get along with his partners. And to be able analyze the extent and quality of those relationships it is necessary to make a conscious self-evaluation by asking the following questions:

Rating:

1) Without a question, not!
2) Probably not.
3) I'm not sure.
4) Probably yes.
5) For sure, yes.

A. Do I dedicate more time observing the positive qualities of people instead of thinking critical thoughts of them?

(1) (2) (3) (4) (5)

B. Do I avoid talking bad about my fellow workers behind their backs?

(1) (2) (3) (4) (5)

C. Do I avoid correcting the little things they do that bother me?

(1) (2) (3) (4) (5)

D. Do I avoid confronting the partners in public?

(1) (2) (3) (4) (5)

E. Am I able to meet the standards of conduct that I insist that others live by?

(1) (2) (3) (4) (5)

F. Am I able to accept with a positive manner the differences of opinion?

(1) (2) (3) (4) (5)

G. Do I avoid name-calling and making fun of my colleagues?

(1) (2) (3) (4) (5)

H. Do I avoid pressuring my colleagues to conform and be subject to my opinions so as to be more open to their conduct and attitudes?

(1) (2) (3) (4) (5)

I. Do I avoid getting upset when my colleagues show different likes and dislikes to mine?

(1) (2) (3) (4) (5)

J. Do I avoid feeling resentful if my colleague and I had a disagreement?

(1) (2) (3) (4) (5)

K. Do I cooperate and help people achieve their goals?

(1) (2) (3) (4) (5)

L. In the agreements do I take advantage of people?

(1) (2) (3) (4) (5)

M. In the talks do I educate with educated arguments?

(1) (2) (3) (4) (5)

N. Do I try to convince with invented or false arguments?

(1) (2) (3) (4) (5)

O. Do I acknowledge the skills of others?

(1) (2) (3) (4) (5)

Evaluation:

Total Points

68 - 75 = Your manner of RELATING is EXCELLENT!

60 - 67 = Your manner of RELATING is ABOVE AVERAGE.

52 - 59 = Your manner of RELATING is AVERAGE.

1 - 51 = You need help in learning how to RELATE.

It is clear that knowing how to relate with one another allows us to work better together. This is useful not only for a person but for the whole team involved. It will bring us more satisfaction and help us to become more sociable, and also teach us to respect the ideas of others and help our colleagues if they need help.

A team will always be more effective than an individual.

A team will always be more effective than an individual. It is important to understand that every individual, as a member of the team, will go through a series of steps while adjusting his relationships.

Specifically, these stages are as follows:

1) **Formation:** In this first stage is when the team is formed and it can produce situations such as anxiety, distrust and even also dependency. On the positive side, they would be factors such as

optimism and willingness to commit to the team's goals and, therefore, to the company itself.

2) **Agitation:** In this stage is when team members begin working as such and that can lead to certain conflicts between them such as criticizing each other for noticing defects and not virtues.

3) **Normalization:** This phase we could say is one in which the members of the group have come to feel like a part of a whole, able to work together and have resolved the conflicts that existed between all of them and that translates into greater comfort and effectiveness.

4) **Fulfillment:** This is where good relationships and harmony reign within the team and that translates to an appropriate, efficient and effective performance in order to achieve the objectives.

The proper functioning of a team depends largely on good relationships. All individuals who are part of the team should strive to connect and achieve the **common goal**. Solidarity, therefore, is essential within the group.

This means that there is no place for personal grandstanding or internal competition that goes against the objectives of the organization. The team, however, must be able to recognize the individual merits of each member. In this way individuals who stand out because of merit will be acknowledged in a healthy manner. All workers want recognition that is given to good performance.

But not only that, it is important that the individual

who is at the helm of the team recognize himself as a member (gear) of the group and engages and is linked to the work. It is essential also to know that he motivate members, to know how to direct them and to know how to improve the qualities and abilities of each. In this way he acts as a gear and brings out the best in each one of the participants, so the results and objectives will be achieved in the best way possible.

Personal relationships are the key to a team, even beyond professional capacity. An individual can learn from his peers and improve his professional skills. In contrast, a person who has a bad relationship with the rest of the team only bring problems and works against the common goals.

Chapter 6

The Interior Comes Before the Exterior

Man's problem is not in developing his skills, but to know how to develop them.

To modify the mind is the most powerful of human virtues because it allows us to realize our dreams. When doubts come about what you want, remember that these things you want you are basing on what you know and not the skills that you are about to develop.

Whatever you want in life, base on what you are about to learn. Because the truth is, what you already know is keeping you where you are now. Close your eyes and see what you really want. Now, say that you have the ability to enhance what you know. Remember that while you have ears and eyes you have the necessary tools to transform your mind and heart.

Individuals improve when they open their conscious mind to new knowledge. Many people fail because they believe they know everything or think they know nothing. When you put a goal for yourself, it will be necessary to have an internal growth. When a person is aware of the growth he needs, then he will seek the knowledge he lacks to achieve that growth. Stephen Covey said, "Internal victories precede the external," anything that is not born in you can be born out of you.

In order for a building to be built, first there must have existed at first an idea in the mind and heart of any investor or builder. Everything that grows in the interior will of a certainty be born on the exterior.

In the world of direct sales or network marketing, the individual is the cornerstone of the organization. Therefore it is important to estimate the quality of our way of being, our way of doing things and our relationships. We can improve these three aspects of our training as leaders, by building, tuning and setting up a good foundation for our organization. To achieve your goals you need to realize that the quality of person you have become is more important than what you've accomplished. And with this condition you will be founding the strongest foundation of your leadership.

Knowing how to achieve your dreams is the basis of your journey. Nothing makes sense if it does not begin with an **understanding**. What we understand we tend to believe. Belief leads to action and action produces results.

People are guided by what they know. Therefore it is essential that they know that their manner of BEING, their manner of DOING, and the way they RELATE are meshed like gears and one aspect affects the other and the three together become the foundation of your achievements.

CHAPTER 7

The Drive Gear

"Only that which is born within you can be born outside of you."

As I explained in my book "Engage", the story of the gear begins with the theory that Archimedes said: "Give me a fulcrum and I will move the earth."

As King Hiero II questioned the statement, Archimedes requested that they load a boat with passengers and cargo that would require many men to pull it out of the water and tie it to the wharf. Archimedes, sitting at a distance in a chair, began gradually pulling on the ends of ropes passing through a pulley system (of wheels) and dragged the boat straight out of the water all by himself.

It is said that Hiero published the next day an edict that from that day on, everything Archimedes said was to be considered true.

What is a GEAR?

Gears are nothing but wheels with teeth. A wheel with teeth is known as a gear, and it is used to transmit power from one component to another. We can speak of "gearing" when movement is generated by gears connected to each other and the system of gears is driven by one particular gear which is connected to a power source. This gear that generates the motion is known and the "**drive gear**". The motor axis starts to move to the active engagement and other gears are set in motion. **This gear has the function of being a mechanism to maximize strength and production.**

So then, the dream, goals or objectives of an individual become a source of fuel and energy that energize the "drive gear". The drive gear is the **BEING**, which puts the **DOING** gear in motion, and this puts the **RELATIONSHIP** gear in motion. This **Linear Gear System** has the function of maximizing the results.

So then, the dream, goals or objectives of an individual become a source of fuel and energy that energize the "drive gear".

Each of these three gears (BEING, DOING, and RELATIONSHIPS), **must be bound, assembled, built, grouped and organized to maximize efficient usefulness, joining forces and motion in an energy transmitting manner.**

That is, the **BEING** is the drive gear to transmit power to the **DOING** and the **RELATIONSHIPS** gears. These three gears running in parallel, generate very good productivity. Depending on the quality or character of BEING to transmit motion will be the effectiveness of DOING and RELATIONSHIPS.

These three gears (BEING, DOING, and RELATIONSHIPS) **are the basic and indispensable elements to maximize results in terms of direct marketing is concerned.** Lets consider this. A gear by itself does not maximize its potential. That is, you can be a great person but if you **DO** nothing, nothing happens. On the other hand, you can DO a lot. But DOING just for the sake of DOING without being aware of what quality you do things will have no results. Still, you can **RELATE** with people in the most efficient way but if you DO nothing else you will not have the results.

The BEING is the drive gear to transmit power to the DOING and the RELATIONSHIPS gears.

There are people hiding in RELATIONSHIPS to avoid putting out any effort. Ladies and gentlemen, a gear alone, that is, the BEING, the DOING, or the RELATIONSHIPS, alone accomplishes nothing. The meshing of these gears is what creates synergy and achieves better results compared to the efforts of just one gear.

So then, we come to understand that the **way of BEING is equivalent to the drive gear, which is the mechanism that drives the DOING gear. And then the DOING gear puts in motion the RELATIONSHIP gear**. These three elements play a fundamental role in the multilevel industry.

I have seen individuals spoil organizations for not giving importance to this concept. In the same way I have seen so-called leaders ignore this linear mechanism and in so doing hinder their fellow partners in the business.

At the beginning when we were starting the business, there was a supposed leader called Epi. He was dishonest. He would say one thing and do another. He concealed the truth. There were times when he displayed a bad attitude when feeling exposed. He was impatient and arrogant, and sometimes even disrespectful. We soon realized his nature of **BEING** and therefore we distrusted him regarding the **DOING**. When we would sponsor someone, we would do our best to hide them from Epi we knew he could humiliate and hurt them with his comments and his way of **RELATING** to them. The group would grow and then get smaller.

It took us some time to realize that the way Epi was **BEING** was affecting his **DOING** and consequently the relationships of the IBOs was seriously affected. New partners would gradually pull away from Epi, and eventually quit.

On a scale of 1 to 10, in relation to his **BEING, DOING** and **RELATIONSHIPS**, I would say Epi would be a 0 in **BEING**, a 2 in **DOING**, and a 3 in **RELATIONSHIPS**. As for his leadership, by multiplying these factors in relation to the linear gear system we would realize that he would have a zero.

That is:

BEING 0 x DOING 2 x RELATIONSHIPS 3 = 0 results

I've also known leaders such as Machuquis, who emphasized a lot the importance of developing the **DOING**. He ignored how important it was to cultivate **BEING** and **RELATIONSHIPS**.

Machuquis had very good achievements. He was very active in regards to List, Contact, Plan, and Follow-up. He was persistent and a dreamer. He planned things according to his convenience. Soon we realized that these achievements were results of cheating and lies.

Machuquis also had a good level in **RELATIONSHIPS**. According to him, he noted the positive qualities of people but would criticize people behind their backs. He would call out small details of behavior that bothered him and from the stage would humiliate those he intended to correct. He avoided confronting the partners in private but instead would do it publicly. He would insist that others keep standards of conduct that he himself broke and did not respect. He would appear to accept with a positive attitude the difference of opinions of others, but in his expression one could see discontent and anger.

Machuquis loved to give nicknames to people and make fun of his colleagues. He demanded that they submit and fit in to his criteria to make it easier to get along with people. He tried to convince people with invented or false arguments.

On a scale of 1 to 10, Machuquis, in **BEING** had a 0, in the **DOING** an 8, and in **RELATIONSHIPS** a 5. As for his leadership, multiplying the three factors which comprise the lineal gear system, we would realize that he ended up with a zero.

In other words:

BEING 0 x DOING 8 x RELATIONSHIPS 5 = 0 results

In the following paragraphs we will give a series of examples of how an individual can begin to grow through the linear gear system of **BEING**, **DOING**, and **RELATIONSHIPS**, by doing a self-assessment in these three areas. The self-assessment that will provide a starting point to the partner. As the leader progresses using the principles illustrated in this book, he will see marked improvements which can be calculated using the graph. In this way a leader can keep his own accounting and ensure that there is no false or deceptive growth, but a real balanced and specific growth in each of his "three gears".

Here's an example of how it works. Let's say that some leader, Panchito, thinks that in his **BEING**, he is more or less a 2. Then, in regards to **DOING**, he thinks he's not really that good because he tends to delay and make excuses to others. So, he gives himself a 1. Finally, Panchito believes he is more or less good at building friendships and maintaining good relations and so he gives himself a modest 3 in regards to **RELATIONSHIPS**. Thus, using the method of solving a mathematical problem: B = 2, D = 1, and R = 3, is solved simply by the formula: 2 x 1 x 3 = 6. Overall rating of Panchito is: 6. This is how Panchito can use his rating results as a personal Evaluation in Effective Leadership.

It is important to understand how this formula measures the leadership:

1000 – 800 = Excellent Leader
800 – 600 = Good Leader
600 – 400 = Average Leader
400 – 200 = Growing Leader
200 – 0 = New Leader

So far, everything is easy. But if we want to genuinely know our own reality, we must be prudent, so as to give certainty and objectivity to give an honest assessment of our own leadership. Because in general, people often exaggerate their assessment of themselves. Always the distance between self-criticism and reality tends to tempt confusion and self-deception.

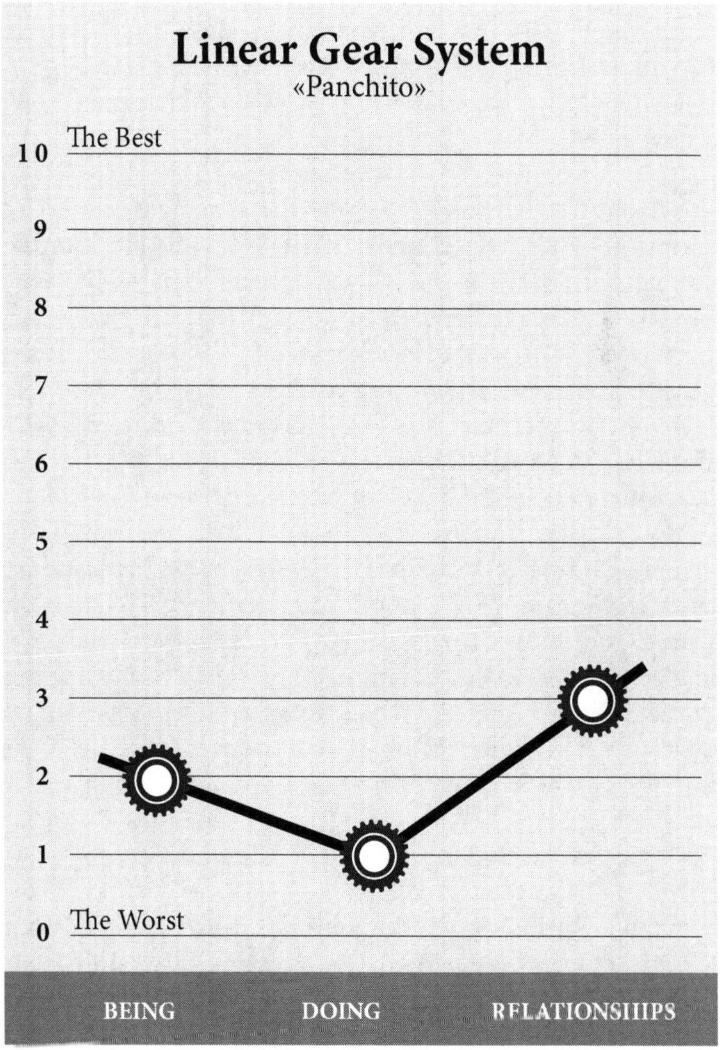

It is when leaders are courageous enough to confront their own diagnosis that they are able to properly take up the challenge and to confront their own prognosis. **Leaders can only improve when they themselves decide to improve.** And they cannot improve, until they know where they are weak and where they are strong. No one can control or alter the past from where their day begins, but they CAN plan to develop what they know and start a new day.

Of course, we must be aware that a new leader, to submit to self-analysis, will usually be weak in all areas, so the overall outcome of the self-assessment will be very low. In these cases, the good news is that they will now be aware of their main weaknesses in each of the "three gears". Therefore, the young leader will locate precisely how much effort is required in each of his gears, of **BEING**, **DOING**, and **RELATIONSHIPS**, and so know where to accentuate efforts to make an impact on his final grade.

For example, let's say that Panchito improves his ability in **DOING** from 1 to 4. Recalculating the total evaluation would give him a final grade of 24 (2 x 4 x 3 = 24) in leadership effectiveness, and to compare with the original grade of 6 when he started, a slight improvement is observed. Obviously, from this it follows that the most important factor was the increase of the multiplier.

2 x 4 x 3=24 en Efectividad de Liderazgo

Obviously, looking at the example, it is considered that the goal of effective leadership will be able to obtain a 10 in **BEING**, 10 in **DOING** and a 10 in **RELATIONSHIPS** in order to achieve the maximum result of 1000 (10 x 10 x 10 = 1000) in our self-evaluation. So moving from a 6 to a 24 is not very impressive. That is why we teach our new leaders that they need patience and perseverance. It takes time and effort to improve step by step from in the areas of **BEING**, **DOING** and **RELATIONSHIPS**, which is the multiplying factor where external difference is transcendental.

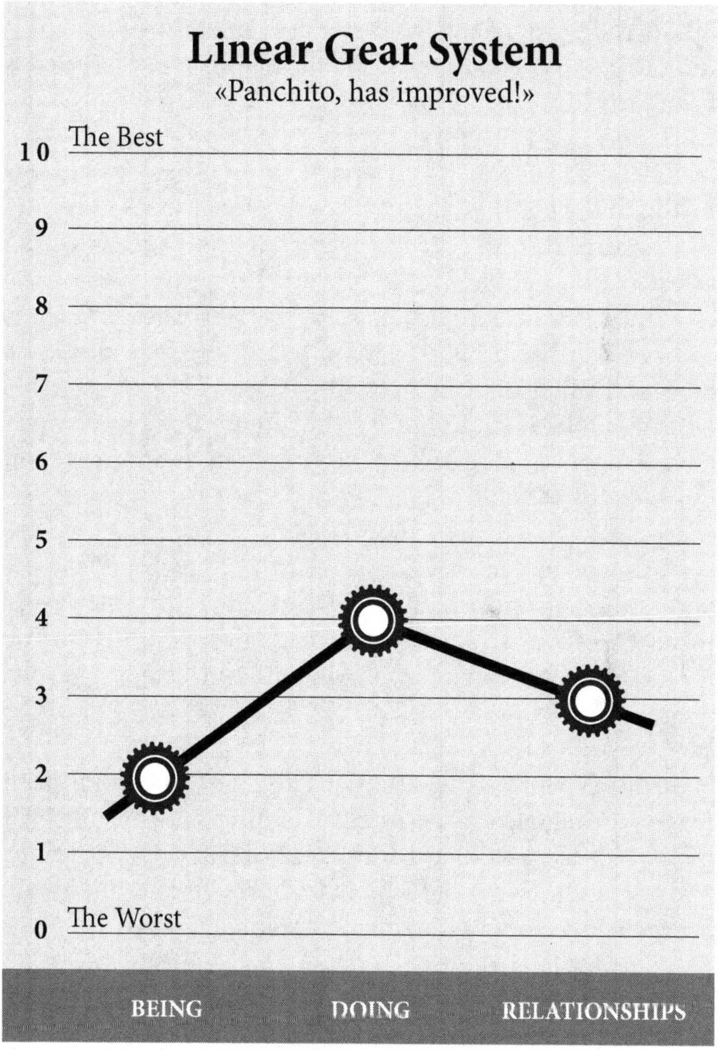

But by using this system of linear gears as a measurement tool of leadership, Panchito has won a victory and has moved from a 6 to a 24, which means a 300% improvement in his Leadership Effectiveness. And look, that is a very important improvement, although from the outside perhaps others can hardly perceive the improvement. However, it is important that Panchito is laying the foundations for his future success.

Likewise, anyone who intends to be a business leader in this business model cannot only be good only in one of these three areas. The linear gear systems shows us that a leader, to become successful, must develop three basic elements that are intertwined and interrelated. Why is this so? Because businesses require a business leader to be constantly interacting with his **BEING**, his **DOING**, and his **RELATIONSHIPS**. In other words, these three gears must have the ability to be linked and related in their interaction in order to get good results.

And when a leader understands the concept of "Gears" and takes full responsibility to grow gradually and evenly in all three areas, it is only a matter of time before the multiplier effect of the improvement and external results are revealed.

In other words, the external will begin to reveal itself when a leader takes responsibility for improving his **BEING**, his **DOING**, and his **RELATIONSHIPS** by conscious effort, taking charge of his personal growth and does what is necessary to strengthen his weaknesses.

Well, when a leader has managed to balance these three profiles in his life he will enjoy a combined effect, which will provide the basis to continue working towards excelling equally in each of the foundational areas of his life. And as he grows through the use of this self-evaluation method, his notoriety will increase as well as his reputation and influence among the people. The compounded effect of the three gears working together produces a powerful result in the leader, in his ability to give the best of his **BEING**, the best of his **DOING**, and the best of his **RELATIONSHIPS**. This compounded effect is what causes a leader to have successful results. Its not something supernatural, much less something magical, but rather something that can be achieved with willpower, decision and perseverance. And this method of self-evaluation called Linear Gear System is a way of demonstrating and measuring improvement and the particular impact of each leader.

No one should cop-out by saying, "Oh, but I wasn't born a leader!" because history has shown us that leaders are not born, they are made! How many times have we seen in this business model everywhere that there are simple people, humble, or natural, that have a tremendous influence on others and they obtain incredible external results that demonstrate the power of their influence. Yes, we have seen this many times, in every generation, and in differing social levels. That is the power of the Drive Gear (**BEING**), the **DOING** gear, and the **RELATIONSHIP** gear, that work together as a whole.

All of the great leaders of history have left inerasable tracks in this world and on their generation, because they used this combined effect when as leaders, they realized that they alone, as strong as they were, as talented as they were, or as rich as they were, they could change nothing, and to them, all transcendental achievements required massive influence on others in their capacity as leaders.

The important thing to celebrate is that this leverage is available to all. It is only required to make the decision to follow this modern process for developing their own leadership, and head for balanced growth in **BEING**, **DOING**, and **RELATIONSHIPS**.

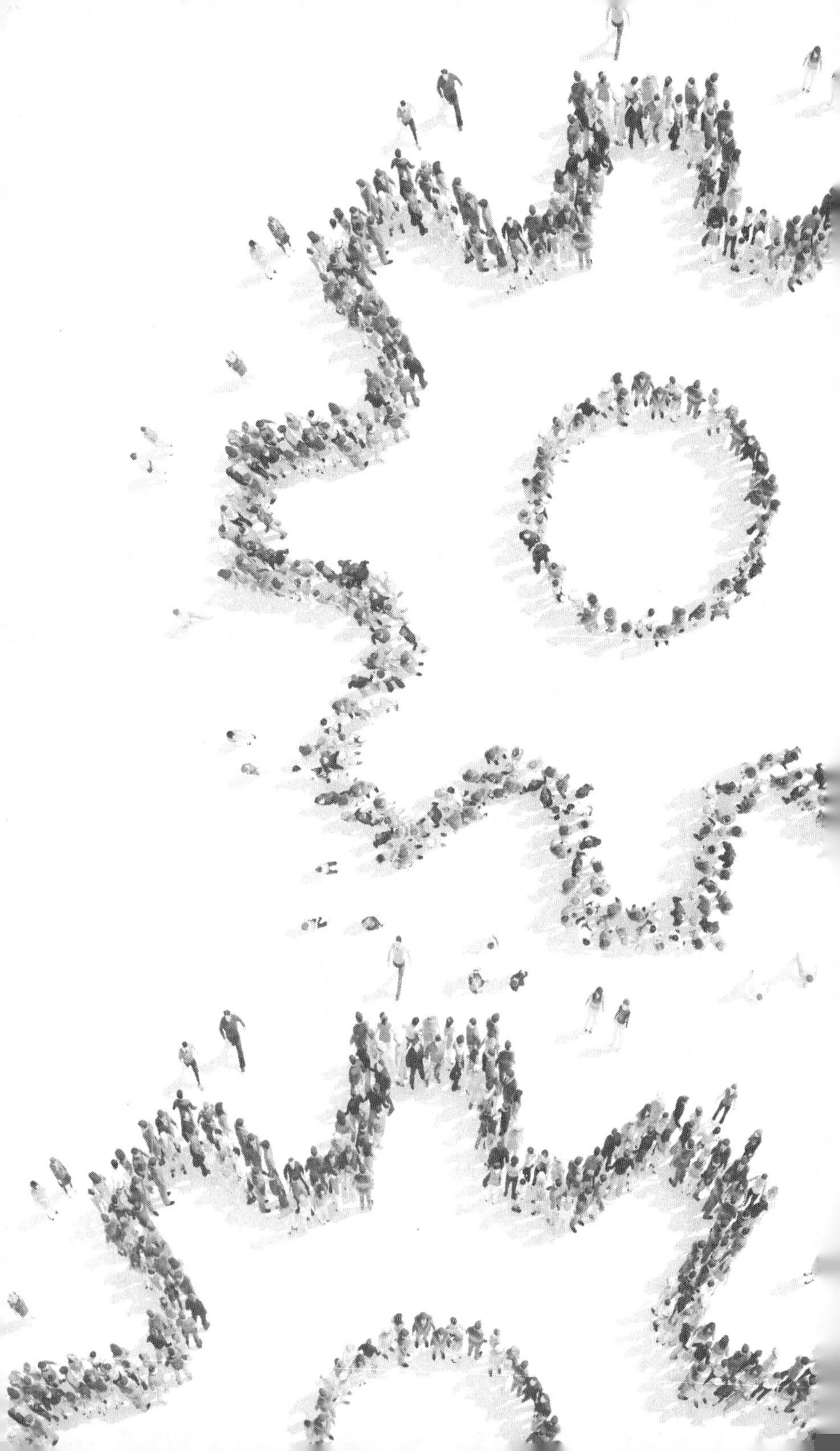

Chapter 8

Summary

What is a **Linear Gear System**? A Linear Gear System is when your **BEING**, your **DOING**, and your **RELATIONSHIPS** are working in synchronized and harmonious manner.

A person can grow externally in money, fame, in business, but if inside everything is not in harmony with that growth, everything will collapse soon or the person will simply live a life with much unhappiness.

Personal growth is not an option for a leader. The Bible tells us that we will never be given more than we can handle. Therefore, if we want more, we must develop the capacity to handle more.

The **Linear Gear System** is a tool we can use to measure the effectiveness of our leadership. That is, it is meant to be a simple method of self-analysis; to measure the effectiveness of our results as we move toward any goal.

So then, lets all of us, every leader and every person take the opportunity to have a look at ourselves, so that we can do an honest self-analysis, and in a concientious manner identify our potential and limitations.

Self-analysis

Observe the following example: **B x D x R= MP**

Being X Doing X Relationships = Maximum Potential

Let's put numbers in this formula. Imagine that the highest Maximum Potential is 1000.

900 - 1000 = Maximum Potential
700 - 900 = Good Potential
500 - 700 = Average Potential
200 - 500 = Growing Potential
200 - 000 = New Leader

We cannot fail to mention here that people need to grow in the three areas simultaneously. When a leader fails to understand this need, he will stagnate in his growth.

A single gear that is energized can move a certain weight, but add more gears and the multiplied effort will compound the results.

A leader who wants to go far in this business model cannot afford to grow only in one quality. He needs to implement the three elements of the **Linear Gear System**.

When a leader understands fully the concept that he needs to grow progressively in these three areas, it is only a matter of time before the results will be revealed to all around him. A leader must understand that he has a potential much greater than he is able to see at this time, and making use of each gear he will be able to work towards personal growth, reach his goals easily and with less effort. Progress is slow when we neglect any

of these three areas. It is time to take responsibility for your leadership and begin to assess and recognize your weaknesses and failings until they become strengths.

Maintaining a balance in the three gears will result in

maximum potential. People should not say, “I was not born to be a leader.” They should never devalue themselves by saying, “I do not have enough opportunities”, or “I have too many flaws.”

According to the concept of the **Linear Gear System**, growth depends on the ability to sensitize your personality, your work, and your way of relating. These three gears are what will lead you to growth. This growth is progressively achieved internally and externally. Leaders are not born, they are made, and that is what we have already explained, but we also wanted to apply that concept and demonstrate it by means of Arquimedes theorem, “Give me a fulcrum, and I will move the world.” **Leaders who fail are not conscious that they can build their growth on this concept of Linear Gear System: BEING, DOING and RELATING.** Each one of these qualities will help you run more effectively towards your dreams.

The three gears in a human, BEING, DOING and RELATING, and interrelated. The dream, the desire to improve oneself, is the fuel that makes the Drive Gear provide power based on BEING.

The three gears in a human, **BEING, DOING** and **RELATING**, are interrelated. The dream, the desire to improve oneself, is the fuel that makes the Drive Gear provide power based on **BEING**. There is no growth based on the **Linear Gear System** without the willpower of the individual and without conscious effort. No one can develop themselves or develop others against their will or without their own effort.

These three elements drive or make possible the improvement of the individual, and they move him to a world of new perspectives. Any blockage of one of these gears will slow down or even destroy the gear system and cause you to lose your progress and your objectives.

When a person develops himself, it results in an increase in his skills which in turn produces better and greater achievements.

However, individuals learn when they open their consciousness to new knowledge. Many people fail because they believe they know everything or think they know nothing.

When a person develops himself, it results in an increase in his skills which in turn produces better and greater achievements.

When we talk about goals, there needs to be growth within a person. When the person is aware of the growth that is needed, then he goes looking for that knowledge. Stephen Covey said, "Internal victories precede external victories."

Nothing that is not born within you can be born out of you. For there to be a building, first there must have been an idea in the mind and heart of any investor or builder. Everything that grows in the interior of a surety will be born on the outside.

One has to reason and accept that what one becomes is more important than what one achieves. And with this condition we will be establishing the strongest foundations of our leadership. Therefore it is important to estimate the quality of our way of being, our way of doing things and our way of relating. These three aspects of our training as leaders we can build, enhance, and adjust as necessary.

It is important to understand how this formula measures the leadership:

1000 - 800 = Excellent Leader
800 - 600 = Good Leader
600 - 400 = Average Leader
400 - 200 = Growing leader
200 - 000 = New Leader

The result of 1000 in effectiveness, we can see it as difficult, but it is not impossible. What you should never do is stop in your search; the fight must persist shortening the gap between where we are and the possibility of achieving the maximum we can dream. We should never be content to believe that we have reached the top because this belief will slow the momentum of progressive rhythm that we carry. Even worse, you could even set us back.

There are many stories of great leaders who managed to have a tremendous influence, and thought that was enough to "sleep on their laurels", neglected their own personal growth then fell dramatically, simply because of their egotism and lack of consideration and concern for themselves and others.

But if it is about stories to tell, it's best to rely on the historical examples of leaders who never gave up in the battles they had to fight, never capitulated in their dreams and hopes of victory, and redoubled their efforts to succeed because they never stopped when they reached the top. From there they looked at many comrades who still needed their leadership and continued without boasting of what they had accomplished, but humbly acknowledged what they still lacked in order to be useful in the growth and progress of others.

We should never be content to believe that we have reached the top because this belief wil slow the momentum of progressive rhythm that we carry.

Here is a brief sketch of one of those leaders of who became known as the "Notorious Hero of the Americas," Don Benito Juarez Garcia.

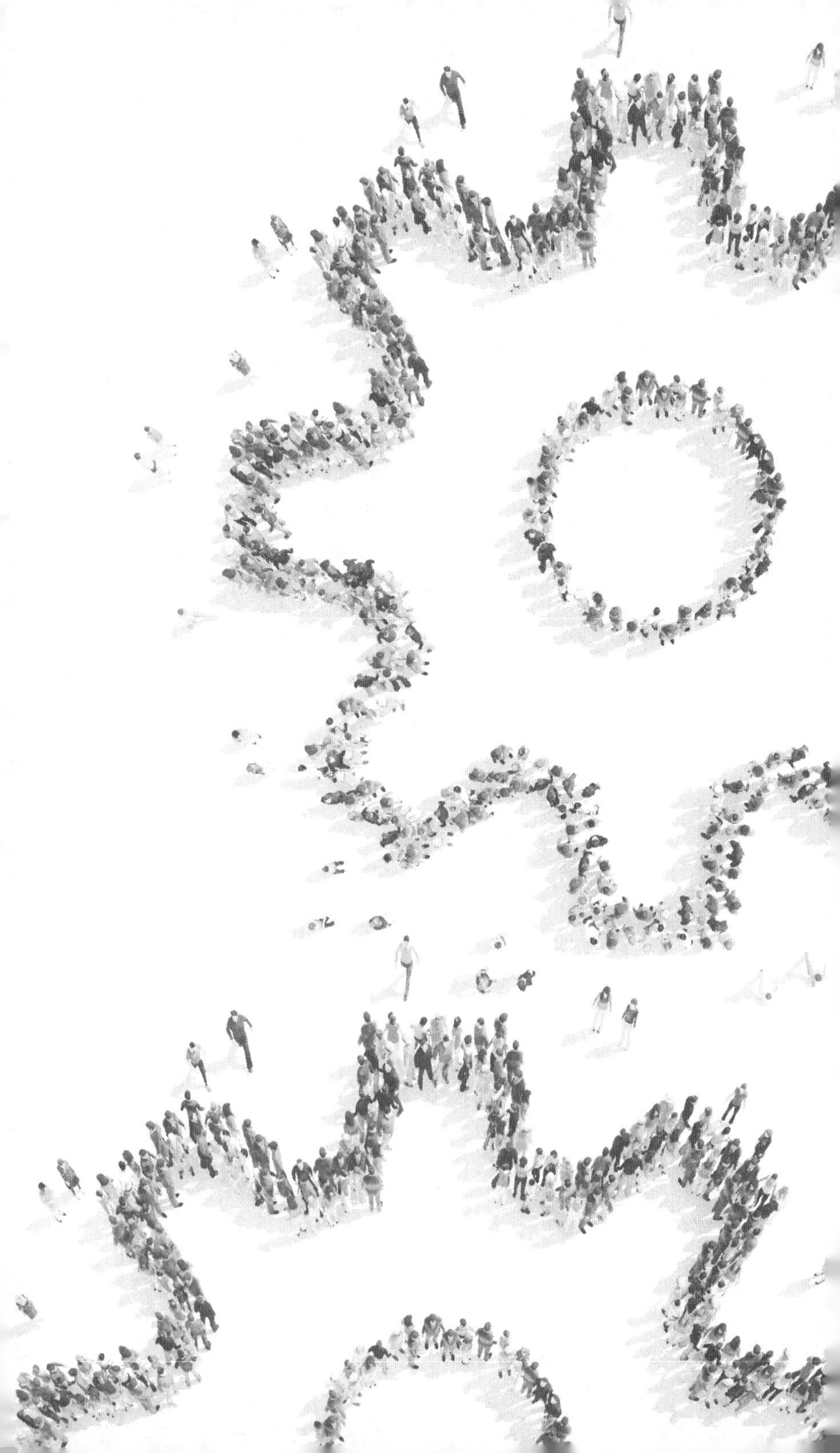

CHAPTER 9

Biographical Sketch

Don Benito Juárez García

«Notorious Hero of the Americas»

Benito Pablo Juarez Garcia, was born on March 21, 1806, in the village of San Pablo Guelatao, Oaxaca, Mexico, located in the tightly packed mountainous region of Mixtec-Zapotec (now Sierra de Juarez). He was the son of Marcelino Juárez and Brigida Garcia, who were, in his words "Indians of the primitive race of the country," and died when Benito was just 3 years age.

He was then raised by grandparents and sisters, Rosa and Josefa, but eventually ended up in the custody of his uncle, Bernardino Juárez who could only think of putting the boy to work in the fields, as farmhand and a shepherd of sheep until he reached the age of 12 years at which time fled to the city of Oaxaca, out of fear, after losing a couple of sheep under his care.

(Those were turbulent times in Europe where social movements were brewing to break the superstitions reminiscent of feudal times and in all of America colonialism and oppression of the Indians was accentuated by subjecting them to ruthless exploitation and condemning them to lack of educational opportunities, to live in the dark ages).

By the time the boy arrived in the city of Oaxaca, he had spent several days on the road, walking barefoot, ragged, hungry and exhausted. He spoke only the native language of Zapotec, and after no small effort, finally located his sister Josefa, who was a servant of a foreign merchant named Maza.

After recounting his adventures of how he had come to arrive at the owners house, he was welcomed as a domestic servant by Mr. Maza. Benito could not read or write, but he insisted that his master teach him words of the Castilian language and in turn he would give the corresponding Zapotec translation. And hereby he obtained the sympathy of Don Antonio Maza, who interceded for Benito before Franciscan priest Antonio Salanueva who graciously accepted him as an apprentice binder.

It was here, having access to printed brochures, and listening to some of their titles and contents that he developed an incredible appetite for knowledge, and right there, in his spare time, he would begin to study and persevere in developing his aspirations of self-improvement. The Franciscan priest was impressed with the character, determination and tenacity of that child, his perseverance in learning, and better chose to process his entry into the seminary in the city.

At the seminary of "Santa Cruz", he completed subjects such as Latin, Philosophy and Theology. But Seminary studies did not satisfy him; he was especially bored theology class during which time he usually slept. Against the wishes of his guardian Salanueva, he left the seminary and entered the profession of Jurisprudence at the Institute of Sciences and Arts of Oaxaca. Some of his teachers there were Free Masons who were impressed by the strong character he exhibited being able to excel in several courses and because of their admiration for him, and the influential relationships he had developed there, this native Indian was nominated to serve as Rector of the Institute, always professing and defending above anything else, his liberal visions and dreams.

On one occasion, he was asked to accept to play the role of a "Greek" character in a theatrical play, because of his very dark Indian skin, but also because part of the script included reciting some verses in Latin. Without much thought, Benito took on the challenge, and in order to feel and get into the character of a Greek, whitened his face with cornmeal, in a manner so grotesquely that everyone laughed at him when he came on stage.

However, with the display during the drama of his gracious attitude, the fact that he could speak perfect Latin with a Roman accent and even mimic the French accent, he was able to greatly influence his relationship with the public and caused the crowd to break out in cheers and thunderous applause thundered! But Benedict did not flinch; he did not let fleeting expressions of glory and honor hinder his ongoing development of his potential.

Already in 1833, with his character and attitude, he won the admiration and respect of his teachers who already recognized him as a true leader, and because of the relationship that he had developed with them, they elected him to a modest position on the council and that same year he was promoted to his first elective office as a local deputy. But he never rested, rather he continued fulfilling all his responsibilities in learning, until he got his release from that Institute in 1834, receiving a Degree in Law.

But the country's conditions were not easy for a liberal and the clerical bourgeoisie did not applaud him for his successes, but rather forced him to flee to Puebla, where he had to work managing some public bathrooms. But he never gave up, and eventually returned to Oaxaca where he was appointed Judge of First Instance.

At the age of 37 he married Margarita Maza, the adopted daughter of his former employer. Then he was named Prosecutor of the Supreme Court of Justice in Oaxaca. His attitudes as leader were giving him more influence and in 1847 he moved to Mexico City as a Federal Deputy, where he learned the inner secrets of the Masonic organization. He joined with the name "William Tell" and formed his own group.

At the time of the US invasion, he was appointed interim governor of Oaxaca, and his actions were characterized by achieving economic and cultural balance of his followers, who were already the vast majority of the people. He doubled the number of school buildings, created the port of Huatulco and built the road connecting it with the capital of Oaxaca. From 5:00a.m. he would set up his desk in public, so that anyone, regardless of their social or economic status, could come talk to him. From there he would go to his regular office and not leave until very late at night.

Upon completion of his term in office, the Institute of Sciences and Arts called for him to return as professor at the school and on his first day, all of the personnel received him with honor, for which he felt most uncomfortable and said, "Free, and for me, the right to think is sacred... Education is fundamental for social happiness; it is the principle on which rests the freedom and the aggrandizement of the people."

One day when he was teaching, he was taken prisoner by certain military personnel sent by the traitor Antonio López de Santa Anna, who exiled him from Veracruz to Cuba, where he worked in a cigar factory.

When he was able to save enough money he went by boat to New Orleans, which we sought the help of fellow Masons and there he met Melchor Ocampo and other Hispanics, with whom he met frequently, in different homes and sometimes in secret, to discuss their political and immigration situation in the United States and to plan a network that would give them economic respite as they were earning miserable salaries and they also discussed their options for returning to Mexico.

From exile, this group supported the famous "Plan of Ayutla" at which time in 1854, the traitor Antonio Lopez de Santa Anna was defeated, and in 1855, Juan Alvarez, upon receiving the presidency of the Republic, named Don Benito Juarez as Minister of Justice and Public Instruction.

Combining his **character** with his **attitude**, he issued and implemented the "Law on Administration of Justice and Organic Law of the courts of this nation", which was law for all the Mexican territory and in one fell swoop eliminated the military and ecclesiastical privileges, deleting the "special courts". This law was the basis for the political and economic separation between "church and state" and whose enactment, cause no small stir amongst religious and political leaders alike, and the President Ignacio Comonfort, did his best to reconcile the interests of conservatives and liberals (colloquially put, he tried to gather the chickens with the eagles).

Conservative critics who supported the Catholic Church took advantage of this scenario, manipulating the press to provoke the complicity of those liberals, and again in 1855, Don Benito Juarezwas arrested, in spite of having been Minister of the Interior and President of the Supreme Court. (Here we may observed that Don Benito's **relationships** were put to the test).

This provoked an ideological and military war. The government became corrupt and President Comonfort humbled himself before Don Benito Juarez, asking for his help, and Don Benito addressed the State of Guanajuato, cradle of independence, where Manuel Doblado was governor at the time, and when he arrived, the surprise was great, their relationship had been well planted, because Manuel Doblado had already rejected Comonfort as president and had proclaimed Don Benito Juarez Garcia as President of the Republic.

As a result of this event, he continued to grow in **character**, **attitude** and **relationships**, enacting progressive legislation and influence that gave rise to the Constitution of 1857. It would be very demonstrative to recount all the times that this leader led the "dreams" of economic and cultural freedom of his followers.

As leader of the republic, from 1858, circumstances pushed him to assume the cause of his followers, undertaking a pilgrimage throughout the country. The first route was in a carriage pulled by horses (he did not have airplanes or cars at his disposal) to Guadalajara, Colima and Manzanillo. He embarked on a boat and crossed the Panama Canal, stopping in Havana with final destination for New Orleans, where the press constantly followed him.

He returned to Veracruz where his wife and children were waiting for him, along with a cheering crowd, but he did not budge, still promoting his character and attitude to optimize his relationships, giving lectures, holding meetings and constantly training different groups to address the challenges of the Catholic clergy and the elite affected by the liberating freedom that this leader infused.

Until he finally achieved the victory, after his pilgrimage across the country as constitutional president while safeguarding against its conservative critics and defeating the French invasion that glorious May 5, 1862, supported by the Zapocoaxtlas Indians, ridiculing the most powerful army of those times. Neither was this heroic deed enough to stop Don Benito; he knew that if he stood still it would hurt his cause, and he was right. The Vatican, the British, French and Spanish governments decreed a spiritual, economic and military "Embargo", against the leadership of Don Benito Juarez.

This shrank his defensive capabilities and so he resumed his pilgrimage through the country by going to Dolores Hidalgo, Guanajuato, where an old man attempted to bow to that leader. But he stopped him saying, "It is I who should I bow to you" and when he asked him how he saw Don Miguel Hidalgo, the old man replied, "He was an extraordinary man". And Benito Juarez replied something like this: "Mexicans now, are known by our attitudes, relating ourselves to his ideals."

Continuing his travels in his carriage, he came to San Luis Potosi, then Monterrey, Saltillo and Chihuahua where he established his leadership, perhaps thinking to be near another great leader, Abraham Lincoln, who could do nothing or little at the time, because the United States was in the middle of a civil war, between the North and the South.

On March 21, 1965, they organized a birthday party for Benito Jaurez, but upon hearing about it, tried to have it cancelled, but the euphoria the list great leader caused was irresistible. So Don Benito ordered that not a penny of government money be spent on this event and that the meeting (about 800 people) be used to retrain all liberal spiritually faint that first drove him to leadership.

But the war dragged on and the itinerary of the pilgrimage of Juarez was repeated again and again through many cities of the Mexican nation. Nonetheless, the European invaders eventually overtook the city of Mexico.

And when the allied forces of the French, British, Spanish and clerical Vatican had already installed Maximilian of Hamburg as "emperor" and supposed that the followers of Benito Juarez had been eliminated, the very day of May 5, 1867, in San Luis Potosi before a crowd of men, women, youth and children, the victory was proclaimed, with the **character** and **attitude** of the leader Don Benito Juarez Garcia and a wealth of **relationships** of many trained leaders, forged in the heat of the battle within his Republican organization.

In that memorable act, Don Benito essentially stated in his speech the following:

"People of Mexico, dear fellow citizens, the bloodshed which the Republic has gone through, can never be forgotten. The blood of your sons, the blood of your husbands, the blood of your fathers, was not shed in vain, because in establishing the Republic (character), freedom is established (attitude), and national sovereignty is strengthened. And the concert (relations) of all nations will admire this people, today, forever and ever and ever.

"Remember this, we can not waver, we must keep going because our reward will be eternal glory and the respect of all peoples and nations who will know that Mexico is no place to look for adventure and brave battle to subdue a people to slavery.

"At this moment, I say to you, Mexicans! Freedom is a reality, freedom is an example to all nations and peoples and I am proud to be the president (leader) of many (leaders) Mexican fighters and our nation today is really mature, today honored, today feared, today brave, today strong, and this date is just the beginning, the beginning of a greatness that will never end (because it will always produce noble leaders).

"It would be wrong to allow ourselves to be disarmed by a superior force, but it would be a terrible tragedy to disarm our children, depriving them of a moral right, who being more courageous, more patriotic and more sacrificing, would assert its value and know to reclaim it some day."

"No appeasement with flawed men and those who have come to be accustomed to do their own will as Moors with no master."

"Men are nothing; principles are everything."

"You can not rule base impulses by a capricious will, but only by being subject to the law."

"You cannot improvise fortunes, nor be given to idleness and dissipation, but rather be devoted assiduously to work, ready to live honestly in modesty."

Here we have the example of a leader who never gave up, never laid down to "sleep on his laurels," believing he had already done enough.